# Scholastic
## Atlas
### of
## Earth

SCHOLASTIC REFERENCE

An imprint of

SCHOLASTIC

Library of Congress Cataloging-in-Publication Data
Scholastic atlas of Earth
p. cm.
Includes index.
1. Earth—Juvenile literature. I. Scholastic Reference (Firm)

QE501.25.S36 2005
550—dc22                          2004052502

ISBN 0-439-67270-8

10 9 8 7 6 5 4 3 2          05 06 07 08 09

Printed in Singapore   46
First printing, November 2005

*Scholastic Atlas of Earth* was created and produced by:

QA International
329, rue de la Commune Ouest, 3e étage
Montréal (Québec) H2Y 2E1 Canada
T 514.499.3000   F 514.499.3010
www.qa-international.com

**Editorial Director**
Caroline Fortin

**Editor-in-Chief**
Martine Podesto

**Editor**
Johanne Champagne

**Editorial Assistants**
Marie-Anne Legault
Stéphanie Lanctôt

**Writer**
Donna Vekteris

**Graphic Designer**
Éric Millette

**Layout**
Jérôme Lavoie
Jean-François Nault

**Art Director**
Anouk Noël
Marc Lalumière

**Illustrators**
Carl Pelletier
Rielle Lévesque
Jean-Yves Ahern
Alain Lemire

**Photo Acquisition**
Nathalie Gignac

**Proofreading**
Veronica Schami Editorial Services

**Geology Consultant**
Christian Lévesque

# Contents

## History of Earth

6    How Earth was formed
8    History of life
10   Fossils

## Inside Earth

14   Earth's structure
16   The soil
18   Rocks
20   Minerals and precious stones
22   Metals and fossil fuels

## Breathtaking landscapes

26   Climatic zones
28   Erosion
32   Water
36   Mountains
38   Caves
40   Glaciers

## Earth's fits of anger

44   Tectonic plates
46   Volcanic eruptions
48   Volcanism
50   Volcanic landscapes
52   Earthquakes
54   Landslides
56   Drought and flooding

## The environment

60   Biosphere and ecosystems
62   Climate change and global warming
64   Deforestation and desertification
66   Sources of pollution

Facts   68
Cartography and terrestrial coordinates   72
Activities   74
Glossary   76
Index   78

# History of Earth

Created in a whirlwind of space dust about 4.6 billion years ago, Earth has not always resembled the planet we know today. Its landscape has been changing constantly throughout its history. Continents and oceans formed and then shifted about; plants and animals appeared and then were replaced by other species. The record of this fascinating evolution lies in sedimentary rocks and their fossils, which tell the story of our planet.

# Once upon a time, a planet...

Five billion years ago, our solar system was an immense cloud of gases and dust. A gigantic shock, perhaps the explosion of a nearby star, made this cloud collapse and spin like a whirlwind. The center of the cloud became more compact, hotter, and brighter, and out of it came a new star, the Sun. As the remaining dust particles continued to revolve around the Sun, they slowly clustered together to form rocks. The rocks crashed into one another, joined together, and became larger rocks. This is how Earth and the solar system's eight other planets formed about 4.6 billion years ago. Our young planet, however, did not at all resemble the one we know today.

## From lava to oceans

During the hundreds of millions of years following its formation, primitive Earth was constantly being bombarded by meteorites, which are rocks that originate in space. The young planet did not yet have an atmosphere, oceans, or continents.

**1.** Young planet Earth was completely covered in a deep layer of burning lava, which is liquid rock, several miles (or kilometers) thick. It did not yet have a solid crust.

**2.** Slowly, the lava covering the surface cooled and began to form Earth's crust.

## GIGANTIC SCARS

Earth's surface was once riddled with craters like the ones found on the Moon, because it was bombarded by meteorites. Over time, these collisions became less and less frequent. Elements like water and wind eventually erased many of the scars, but the most recent ones still exist. A 65-million-year-old crater that measures 125 mi (200 km) across has been discovered off the coast of Mexico. Some scientists think that the giant meteorite that dug this crater played an important part in the disappearance of the dinosaurs!

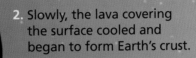

**3.** Over time, a primitive crust formed over the entire planet. Numerous volcanoes marked Earth's surface, spitting out enormous amounts of water vapor and toxic gases that created an unbreathable atmosphere.

**4.** As it cooled, the water vapor in the primitive atmosphere was transformed into thick clouds. Then, for thousands of years, extremely heavy rains fell from the clouds to the planet. This flood of water created Earth's first ocean!

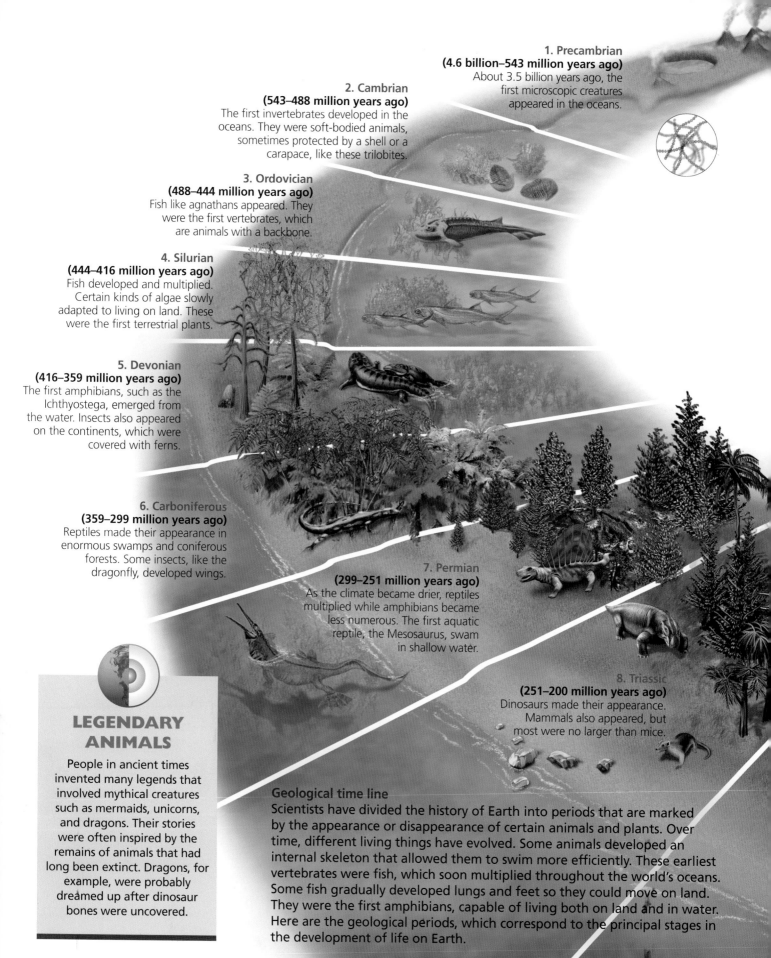

**1. Precambrian**
**(4.6 billion–543 million years ago)**
About 3.5 billion years ago, the first microscopic creatures appeared in the oceans.

**2. Cambrian**
**(543–488 million years ago)**
The first invertebrates developed in the oceans. They were soft-bodied animals, sometimes protected by a shell or a carapace, like these trilobites.

**3. Ordovician**
**(488–444 million years ago)**
Fish like agnathans appeared. They were the first vertebrates, which are animals with a backbone.

**4. Silurian**
**(444–416 million years ago)**
Fish developed and multiplied. Certain kinds of algae slowly adapted to living on land. These were the first terrestrial plants.

**5. Devonian**
**(416–359 million years ago)**
The first amphibians, such as the Ichthyostega, emerged from the water. Insects also appeared on the continents, which were covered with ferns.

**6. Carboniferous**
**(359–299 million years ago)**
Reptiles made their appearance in enormous swamps and coniferous forests. Some insects, like the dragonfly, developed wings.

**7. Permian**
**(299–251 million years ago)**
As the climate became drier, reptiles multiplied while amphibians became less numerous. The first aquatic reptile, the Mesosaurus, swam in shallow water.

**8. Triassic**
**(251–200 million years ago)**
Dinosaurs made their appearance. Mammals also appeared, but most were no larger than mice.

## LEGENDARY ANIMALS

People in ancient times invented many legends that involved mythical creatures such as mermaids, unicorns, and dragons. Their stories were often inspired by the remains of animals that had long been extinct. Dragons, for example, were probably dreamed up after dinosaur bones were uncovered.

**Geological time line**
Scientists have divided the history of Earth into periods that are marked by the appearance or disappearance of certain animals and plants. Over time, different living things have evolved. Some animals developed an internal skeleton that allowed them to swim more efficiently. These earliest vertebrates were fish, which soon multiplied throughout the world's oceans. Some fish gradually developed lungs and feet so they could move on land. They were the first amphibians, capable of living both on land and in water. Here are the geological periods, which correspond to the principal stages in the development of life on Earth.

# The explosion of life

The earliest forms of life appeared in the warm oceans of our young planet less than a billion years after its creation. They were similar to modern-day bacteria, the simplest life-form that exists. Little by little, the first algae and microscopic creatures appeared in the oceans. Using the Sun's energy and carbon dioxide to make their food, algae generated a gas called oxygen, which began to build up in the primitive atmosphere. Some of the oxygen was transformed into a layer of gas called ozone, which protects living things from the Sun's dangerous radiation. This process caused a biological revolution, with animals and plants becoming more complex, adopting different forms, taking over the oceans and the continents, and changing the face of our planet. This is why the history of Earth and the history of living things are closely linked.

**11. Paleogene (66–23 million years ago)**
Small mammals took advantage of the disappearance of the dinosaurs. They grew larger and many new species appeared. The ancestors of whales reconquered the oceans and the first great apes appeared.

**12. Neogene (23 million years ago until today)**
Mammals and birds became the dominant groups. The first humans appeared.

**9. Jurassic (200–146 million years ago)**
Dinosaurs ruled Earth. Some reptiles changed into birds. The first flowering plants appeared.

**10. Cretaceous (146–66 million years ago)**
Many new kinds of flowering plants appeared. At the end of this period, three-quarters of all species disappeared, including dinosaurs, probably as a result of the impact of a huge meteorite.

# Earth's archives

To reconstruct the story of life, scientists turn to fossils. They are the clues left behind by living things that died a long time ago. Examples of fossils include the imprint of a leaf or a footstep, the skeleton of a dinosaur, or an insect trapped in amber. Amber is the hardened resin of coniferous trees. These traces or remains of living organisms are marvelous witnesses to the past. Besides providing proof that life has existed on Earth for a very long time, they reveal how different forms of life evolved and were transformed over time. They also help paleontologists, the scientists who specialize in the study of fossils, to reconstruct the principal stages in the history of life and to learn more about the plants, animals, and even different landscapes that have marked it.

## A LIVING FOSSIL

Most prehistoric animals disappeared long ago and only exist in the form of fossils. There are a few exceptions, however, and the most spectacular one is the coelacanth (pronounced see-la-kanth). It is a primitive fish that appeared on Earth 350 million years ago. Scientists believed the coelacanth had long been extinct until they discovered a live one in 1938 off the coast of South Africa!

Many fossils are marine animals that died and were rapidly covered in sediment before they could decompose and disappear. Sediment is made up of waste of all kinds—including remains of dead organisms—that is continuously being deposited at the bottom of seas and lakes. Over time, many layers of sediment build up, harden, and transform into sedimentary rock. Every layer may contain fossils belonging to a specific period of time. Here are the three principal stages in the formation of a fossil.

See activity p. 75

1. A mollusk dies and lies on the ocean floor. Its body rapidly decomposes, but its shell, which is harder, is preserved.

2. Bit by bit, sediment covers the shell and hardens. The shell is now trapped in the sedimentary rock.

3. After millions of years, movements in Earth's crust or digging by paleontologists may bring the fossil back to the surface.

### The deeper, the older

Scientists have ways of finding out a fossil's age, even when there are no written records. The simplest method is based on observing different layers of sediment. Over time, old sediment is covered by new sediment, building up into layers called strata. Each layer represents a separate geological time period. The sediment lying closest to the surface is usually from the most recent period. This means that the deeper a fossil lies, the older it is. When geological accidents upset the strata, scientists assume that the layers containing the same kind of fossils are from the same period.

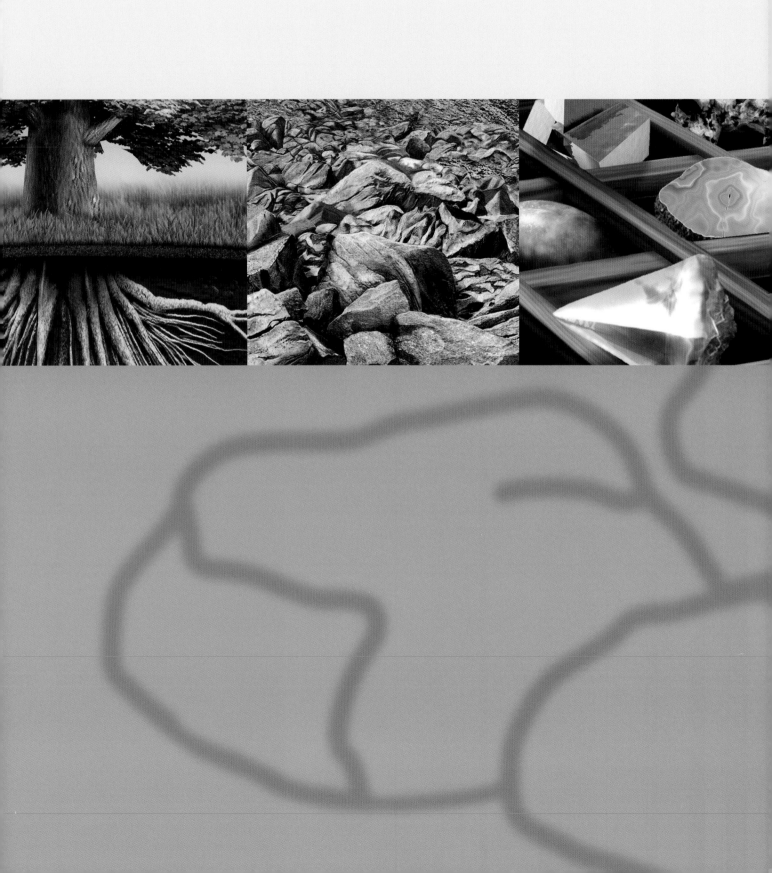

# Inside Earth

Deep inside the planet is a world where extreme pressure and unimaginably hot temperatures rule. In this mysterious environment, matter is turned into an amazing variety of minerals and rocks. Recycled by nature and submitted to processes lasting millions of years, rocks are constantly being transformed. Rocks and minerals are linked to our daily lives because of their use in so many of the objects that surround us.

# At the heart of the planet

All we see of Earth is a thin layer of rock called the crust. This top layer forms the continents and the ocean floor. Only a very small portion of the planet consists of crust. If Earth were compared to an egg, its outermost layer would be no thicker than the eggshell! Except for the rocks lying on the planet's surface and those coming from the insides of volcanoes, no one has ever managed to see what lies under the crust. However, scientists do know what the planet's interior looks like. They have studied the waves that accompany earthquakes and found that these waves move differently, depending on the materials through which they must travel.

**Earth's inner structure**
Scientists have been able to determine the layout of Earth's inner structure. They discovered our planet was made up of several distinct layers.

**The inner core**
Located at the center of Earth, the internal core measures approximately 1,500 miles (2,400 km) in diameter. Despite the intense heat, the iron and nickel in the core remain solid. The innermost part of Earth is as hot as the surface of the Sun. Its temperature is over 10,800°F (6,000°C).

**The external core**
This extremely hot layer consists mostly of two liquid metals, iron and nickel. It measures about 1,400 miles (2,300 km) in depth. The movements of this metallic layer create the electrical energy that is responsible for the magnetic field surrounding Earth.

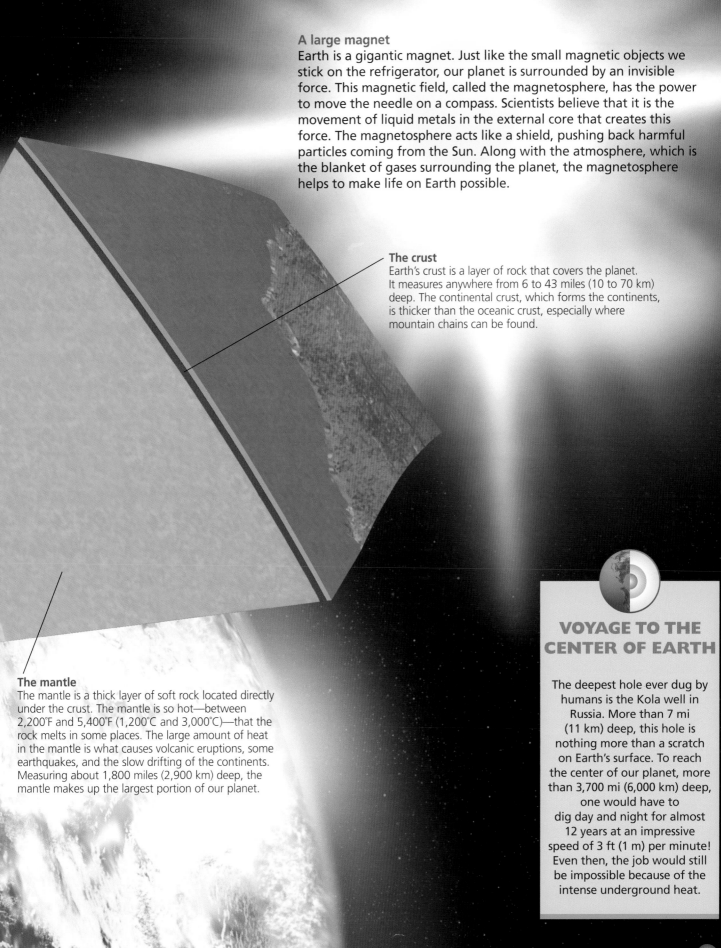

**A large magnet**
Earth is a gigantic magnet. Just like the small magnetic objects we stick on the refrigerator, our planet is surrounded by an invisible force. This magnetic field, called the magnetosphere, has the power to move the needle on a compass. Scientists believe that it is the movement of liquid metals in the external core that creates this force. The magnetosphere acts like a shield, pushing back harmful particles coming from the Sun. Along with the atmosphere, which is the blanket of gases surrounding the planet, the magnetosphere helps to make life on Earth possible.

**The crust**
Earth's crust is a layer of rock that covers the planet. It measures anywhere from 6 to 43 miles (10 to 70 km) deep. The continental crust, which forms the continents, is thicker than the oceanic crust, especially where mountain chains can be found.

**The mantle**
The mantle is a thick layer of soft rock located directly under the crust. The mantle is so hot—between 2,200°F and 5,400°F (1,200°C and 3,000°C)—that the rock melts in some places. The large amount of heat in the mantle is what causes volcanic eruptions, some earthquakes, and the slow drifting of the continents. Measuring about 1,800 miles (2,900 km) deep, the mantle makes up the largest portion of our planet.

## VOYAGE TO THE CENTER OF EARTH

The deepest hole ever dug by humans is the Kola well in Russia. More than 7 mi (11 km) deep, this hole is nothing more than a scratch on Earth's surface. To reach the center of our planet, more than 3,700 mi (6,000 km) deep, one would have to dig day and night for almost 12 years at an impressive speed of 3 ft (1 m) per minute! Even then, the job would still be impossible because of the intense underground heat.

# Beneath our feet

The ground we walk on is swirling with life. It is home to plants and small burrowing animals like ants, moles, and earthworms, and countless microscopic creatures. Along with mushrooms, these microorganisms help to decompose dead animals and plants and turn them into humus, a natural fertilizer that enriches the soil. Natural forces like wind and water break down surrounding rock, and add pebbles and minerals to the soil. Last but not least, the soil contains water and air, which plants and animals need to survive. Without soft, moist, nourishing soil, plants could not grow. Our atmosphere would be unbreathable without green plants, which release oxygen into the air that we breathe. In short, our rocky continents would be almost lifeless if Earth's crust were not partly covered in soil.

### The destruction of soil
It can take more than a century for water, wind, and microscopic creatures to produce a layer of soil less than .5 inch (1 cm) thick. It only takes a few years of bad soil management by humans, however, to destroy it completely. Chemical products such as pesticides, as well as industrial wastes, harm organisms in the soil. Growing the same plants year after year uses up important minerals in the soil. Cutting down all the trees in a forest also damages the soil, which becomes more exposed to wind and rain. Without the roots of the trees to hold it in place, the soil is easily carried away. Human beings often have the power to preserve or destroy the soil covering our planet.

## Layers of soil

Soil varies a great deal depending on the climate, the features of the landscape, and the vegetation covering it. While the soil in most forests is thick and rich in humus, it is thin in mountainous areas. In spite of the differences that have been observed in various kinds of soils, soil specialists have identified several common layers, called horizons.

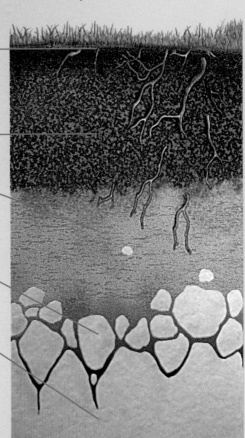

**0 Horizon**
The soil on the surface contains many animals and plant roots. It is mainly composed of humus, a nutritious material that is easy to recognize by its black color.

**A Horizon**
The second layer is composed of dark and fertile soil that is also rich in humus.

**B Horizon**
This horizon, also called subsoil, contains less humus than the layers that cover it. It is rich with small mineral particles that vegetation needs for growing.

**C Horizon**
Lacking in humus, this layer of ground consists of fragments of rock that come from the layer underneath.

**D Horizon**
This layer, also called consolidated rock, forms a rocky base. Consolidated rock is gradually crushed by natural elements like water, freezing temperatures, or the passage of glaciers. This action helps to release important minerals into the other layers of soil.

# A rocky planet

Earth's crust is entirely made up of different kinds of rocks. Although they may appear solid and indestructible, rocks change continuously over time, forming, deforming, and transforming into other kinds of rock. They may be pushed deep inside the planet only to resurface later on. In this way, rocks are recycled by nature, in a complex process that may last millions of years. Some rocks, like the very first ones that appeared on Earth, were formed from magma, a fiery liquid rock buried in the planet's mantle. Some formed out of other kinds of rocks that already existed.

**The origins of rocks**

Many rocks form deep inside Earth. Some are made of magma that has cooled down and solidified. These are called igneous rocks. On the surface, rocks slowly crumble as they are battered by wind, ice, and water. The rock fragments are washed into rivers, lakes, or oceans, where they sink to the bottom and combine with the remains of animals and plants. Over time, the fragments and remains bond together and harden to form sedimentary rocks. Igneous and sedimentary rocks sometimes sink slowly into the ground, where they are crushed, heated, and deformed by the weight and movement of Earth's crust. They are transformed into a third type of rock, called metamorphic rock.

Rocks are combinations of one or more minerals, which are nonliving solid substances produced by nature. The huge variety of rocks can be divided into three general categories: sedimentary, igneous, and metamorphic, which comes in many different forms.

### Granite
Granite is an igneous rock that is extremely hard and durable. Pink granite is often used in the construction of monuments and buildings.

### Limestone
Limestone is a sedimentary rock that forms at the bottom of oceans. It is mainly composed of the shells of very tiny marine animals. This is why limestone often contains fossils.

### Marble
Heat or pressure can transform limestone into marble, a metamorphic rock of great value that is often white and streaked with swirling patterns of different colors.

### Basalt
Basalt is an igneous rock that forms when magma rises to Earth's surface. There it erupts from volcanoes in the form of lava and hardens very quickly on contact with the air or water.

### Slate
Slate is a metamorphic rock that is easy to separate into flakes or sheets. It may be black, gray, or green. Among other things, slate is used on roofs and blackboards.

### Rock salt
Rock salt is a crumbly, sedimentary rock that forms when seawater evaporates and leaves a deposit of salt behind. The table salt we use in cooking sometimes comes from this kind of rock.

## A ROCK THAT FLOATS

Pumice stone is light and brittle with a spongy texture. It is often used to soften the skin of the feet and hands. This igneous rock is riddled with tiny air pockets because the lava that formed it was full of gases. Pumice is so light that it can do what no other rock can: float on water!

# Earth's jewels

Most minerals on Earth are formed when magma rises from the depths of the planet to the surface and then cools. Crystals form from chemical elements present in the liquid rock, somewhat like the way rain turns into snow crystals in the cold. Over time, the structure of some minerals changes under high pressure or high temperatures, producing new kinds of minerals in the process. More than 3,500 different minerals have been discovered so far. Most of them combine to form rocks, like the quartz, feldspar, and mica found in granite. The rarest and most beautiful may be turned into jewelry. This family of minerals, called gems, groups together some 50 different semiprecious stones, including agate, opal, and jade, and four precious stones. These most highly prized gems are diamond, ruby, sapphire, and emerald.

White quartz

Malachite

Feldspar

Emerald

Graphite

See table p. 68

## A REAL GEM

The pearl is one of the gems most favored by jewelers. Unlike other gems, however, pearls do not come from rocks, but from animals! These small, hard, shiny beads are manufactured by pearl oysters. A pearl forms when a foreign object, such as a grain of sand, gets into an oyster's shell. The creature protects itself by secreting a substance called nacre, which coats the irritating bit of sand in several layers. About one in every 100 oysters is hiding a pearl!

### Daily minerals

The minerals in rocks are essential to our lives. They make up many of the objects and materials we use every day. The calcite found in limestone, for example, is used to manufacture cement and asphalt for roads. The minerals in clay are used for making ceramics, bricks, and pottery. There is fluorite in toothpaste, graphite in pencils, talc in cosmetics, and silica in glass, mirrors, and computer chips. Other minerals include the stones used to make jewelry.

Mica

Pyrite

Agate

Jade

Calcite

Talc

Granite

Pink quartz

Fluorite

## Identifying minerals

Geologists are scientists who study the materials that make up the planet. To identify and classify the minerals in rocks, geologists examine a number of features, such as hardness, transparency, form and structure, color, streak color, and sparkle.

### Hardness
It is possible to identify a mineral by its hardness. Some minerals like talc are soft and can be scratched with a fingernail. Other minerals like diamonds are the opposite. Even a knife cannot scratch them.

### Transparency
A mineral can be identified by its transparency. Quartz, for example, is sometimes completely transparent; that is, one can see through it. Copper is opaque. It is impossible to see through.

### Form and structure
Many minerals can be identified according to their outer appearances or internal structures. Hematite may look like small balls. Pyrite's internal structure is the shape of a cube, while the form of the emerald is hexagonal, or six-sided.

### Color
Some minerals can be easily identified by their color. Malachite, for example, is always green. On the other hand, minerals like quartz come in a wide variety of colors, including white and pink.

### Streak color
If the color of a mineral is not always a reliable clue, the color of its streak is. The streak is a powdery line left by a mineral when it is scraped on a porcelain plate. A mineral may come in a wide variety of colors, but the color of its streak almost never changes.

### Sparkle
Sparkle is the twinkle and reflection of light on a mineral. Some minerals like gold have a brilliant metallic sparkle, while others like quartz have a glassy sparkle. Jade has a somewhat greasy sparkle, as if it were covered in oil.

# Treasures hidden in the rocks

Some of the materials hidden in Earth's crust are extremely useful to human beings. People dig hundreds, even thousands, of feet (or meters) underground to find them. They include metals like gold, iron, and aluminum, along with fossil fuels like coal, oil, and natural gas. Fossil fuels are an important source of energy. Metals are valuable as well. Most of them are hidden inside rock, which is known as ore, and are combined with a variety of other elements. Today's advanced extracting and refining methods help mining companies obtain a wide variety of metals. Unfortunately, extracting metals and fossil fuels from underground cannot be carried out without scarring the landscape and upsetting the delicate balance of natural habitats.

**How fossil fuels are created**
Sometimes very large amounts of plants or tiny marine organisms become buried in sediment. Over time, they sink deep into Earth's crust, where they are compressed and heated by the planet's weight and high underground temperatures. After millions of years, these plant remains and dead tiny animals are transformed into fossil fuels. Forests that have been buried for millions of years turn into coal, while microscopic marine organisms turn into oil and natural gas. These highly combustible fuels are used for heating, producing electricity, and running vehicles such as cars.

Most metals are hard, shiny, and strong. They are also very good conductors of heat and electricity. Metals are often mixed with other metals to form alloys. When copper and tin are mixed together, for example, the result is bronze, an alloy that is more solid and resistant than either of the two metals on their own. It is because of these many qualities that metals are used for so many different purposes.

### Aluminum
Both light and strong, aluminum is used in the manufacturing of airplanes, cars, aluminum foil, and compact discs. It is extracted from an ore called bauxite.

### Silver
Silver is a soft metal that is easy to bend and work with. Silver is used in photography, jewelry, ornaments, and electrical equipment.

### Gold
Like silver, gold is used in jewelry, and also as a contact in electrical switches. Because gold is rare, it is also very expensive.

### Copper
Copper is an excellent electrical conductor. It is used for making cooking pots, plumbing pipes, musical instruments, and electrical wires and cables.

### Iron
Strong and bendable, iron is the most widely used metal in the world. It can be turned into wrought iron or into steel, a very strong alloy used in the construction of bridges. Iron is often extracted from an ore called hematite.

### Mercury
Mercury is the only metal that is liquid at room temperature. Because it expands in heat, mercury is used in thermometers.

## MAKING GOLD

During the Middle Ages, some people dreamed of transforming ordinary metals like lead into gold. They never succeeded. It is now theoretically possible for modern physics to manufacture gold but, surprisingly, nobody has ever succeeded in doing it! And even if they did, there would be one drawback: The process of making artificial gold would cost more than the real thing!

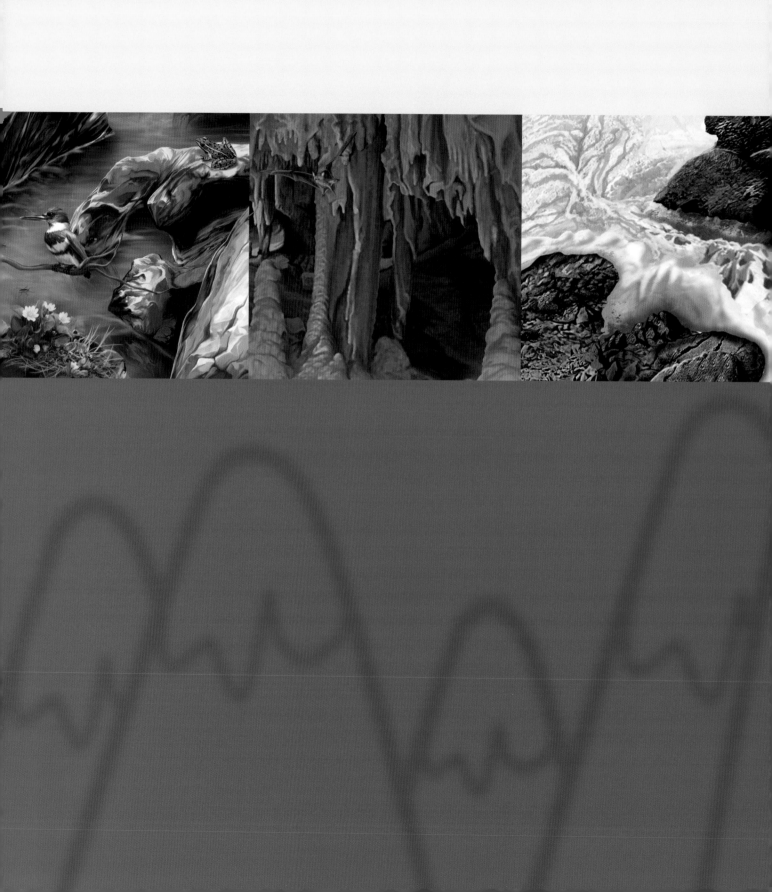

# Breathtaking landscapes

While mountains are formed under the pressure of powerful underground forces, the rest of Earth's landscape tends to change much more gradually. Due to the powers of erosion, valleys are being dug, mountain peaks are being rounded off, and caves are opening up. Through the slow but steady action of water, wind, and ice, erosion sculpts an astonishing variety of landscapes.

# Climates of the world

Climate is the particular condition of the atmosphere at a certain place on Earth. It is the long-term weather of that area. Earth's various regions have very different climates in terms of temperature, precipitation, humidity, and wind. Climatic zones are areas characterized by similar climates. Their distribution on the surface of the planet is dictated mainly by latitude, or distance from the equator. Because of Earth's shape—a gigantic ball that is very slightly flattened—each region of the planet is not equally heated. Countries near the equator are hit directly by the Sun's rays, so they have warm climates. On the other hand, areas located near the North and South Poles get the Sun's rays more indirectly, so they have much colder climates. The climate of a region influences its landscape, plant life, and animal inhabitants. It is therefore responsible for the different "faces" of the planet.

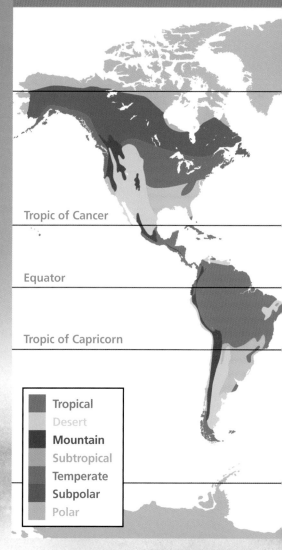

Tropic of Cancer

Equator

Tropic of Capricorn

Tropical
Desert
Mountain
Subtropical
Temperate
Subpolar
Polar

### HOT AND COLD

Earth has a great range in temperatures, with a difference of more than 165°F (90°C). The hottest place on the planet is Dallol, in Ethiopia, with an annual average temperature of 93.9°F (34.4°C). The coldest place is Polus Nedostupnosti, also called the Inaccessible Pole, in Antarctica, with an average temperature of −72°F (−57.8°C). But Vostok, also located in Antarctica, deserves the record for the lowest temperature ever. On July 21, 1983, the temperature dropped to −128.6°F (−89.2°C)!

**Tropical climate**
The tropical zone is located on either side of the equator. The temperature is very high due to regular sunshine all year long. The high and constant humidity favors the development of dense tropical forests. On the edge of the tropics, the climate becomes drier.

**Polar climate**
Near the Poles, temperatures are extremely cold, and the air is so dry that snowfall is rare. In the centers of Antarctica and Greenland, the ground remains frozen and covered with a thick ice cap throughout the year.

# Main climatic zones

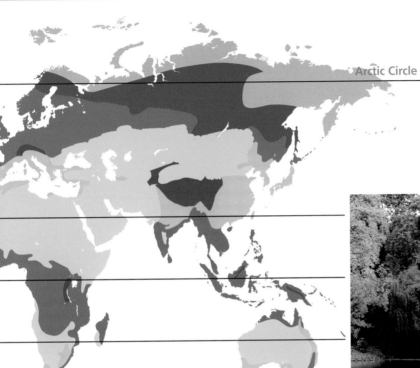

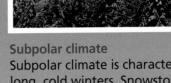

## Subpolar climate
Subpolar climate is characterized by very long, cold winters. Snowstorms here are accompanied by cold, powerful winds. Summers are short and rather cool. Rain, which is infrequent, falls mainly during this season.

## Temperate climate
The climate of the temperate regions has relatively mild conditions and a cycle of four distinct seasons.

Arctic Circle

Antarctic Circle

## Subtropical climate
The subtropical climate is marked by mild winters, hot summers, and heavy rainfall.

## Mountain climate
In mountain climates, temperatures drop and vegetation becomes more sparse as altitude rises. The climate also depends on the slope. In alpine valleys, the slopes facing the Sun receive more sunlight and are warmer than the slopes facing away from the Sun.

## Desert climate
All desert regions have little precipitation (rainfall), barren landscapes with sparse vegetation, and a big difference in daytime and nighttime temperatures.

# Sculpting the landscape

The different landscapes that surround us do not last forever. Spectacular phenomena like volcanic eruption or flooding can change the geography in dramatic ways. It is mainly erosion, however, that is responsible for slowly altering Earth's features. The term "erosion" comes from the Latin *erosio*, which means "gnawing away." Erosion is the slow process of eating away, transforming, and leveling rock and earth. It is a cycle that begins when surface materials are removed, as when bits of rock break off from Earth's crust. The cycle continues with the movement of loose rock and soil particles that can eventually gather to form sediment. In the end, many factors, such as rain and wind, can wear down even the hardest rock. Over time, these natural forces slowly erode Earth's features and gradually transform its landscapes.

### Different types of erosion

Water, wind, and ice are the main natural forces responsible for erosion. They can alter the landscape through two different processes: a chemical process, which attacks the minerals in rock, or a mechanical process, which wears down the rock itself. Other factors, such as animals and plants, do their part to remodel Earth's features. The roots of trees, for example, work their way into small cracks in rock. As the roots grow, they split the rock apart. Humans can trigger phenomena that cause erosion by building roads, for example, or by cutting down forests, leaving bare soil exposed to wind and rain.

### Erosion by waves

As they hit the coast day after day, waves sculpt cliffs. The rock becomes fragile due to the effects of water and sea salt and is altered by the constant impact of sea swell and tides. As the waves carve into the cliffs bit by bit, the cliffs may collapse. Waves are also responsible for carrying sand to and from beaches. Waves can make a coast recede as much as 6 feet (2 m) a year!

### Erosion by a watercourse

In mountains as well as on flat land, a river can dig into the ground and tear away material from its banks and riverbed, which is the space it occupies. This is called fluvial erosion. Stones in the riverbed detach themselves, roll over one another, and break up into smaller bits. As the bits of stone slowly make their way toward the sea, they act as an abrasive to the land, wearing it down as they rub against it. In this way, rivers dig the valleys through which they run.

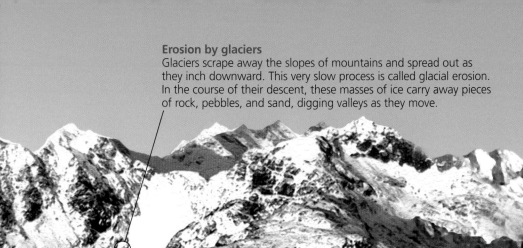

**Erosion by glaciers**
Glaciers scrape away the slopes of mountains and spread out as they inch downward. This very slow process is called glacial erosion. In the course of their descent, these masses of ice carry away pieces of rock, pebbles, and sand, digging valleys as they move.

## IT'S RAINING ACID!

Rainwater forms a natural acid when mixed with carbon dioxide. When rainwater falls on limestone, it dissolves the rock and can create gigantic caves inside it. In polluted areas, other kinds of acid caused by industrial gases are often added to the natural acids already in rain. Acid rain also eats away at the stones of ancient human-made monuments, such as the pyramids, as well as the granite of modern skyscrapers.

**Erosion by frost**
The volume of water, which is the amount of space it takes up, increases by about 10 percent when it freezes. If this transformation takes place in the narrow crack of a rock, the rock is put under enormous pressure—enough pressure to make it shatter. Going from freezing to thawing causes water in the rock to expand and contract, and in the end splits it apart.

**Erosion by seeping water**
Water streaming along the ground moves particles of earth and gradually digs ravines. Water seeping into the ground hollows out caves and underground rivers.

**Erosion by rain**
Rainwater absorbs large quantities of carbon dioxide, a gas from the atmosphere. It may also contain industrial gases like sulfur dioxide, which is produced by the burning of fossil fuels. Rainwater and the chemicals that are dissolved in it have the power to change the makeup of the different minerals in the ground, as is the case with calcite found in limestone. The wearing down by rain is called pluvial erosion.

**Erosion by wind**
The action of the wind has a great impact on dry regions. Rocky particles, soil, or grains of sand exposed to wind are gradually carried away. Wind sculpts rock, carving its features bit by bit. This is called eolian erosion. For the wind to act this way, however, it needs plenty of empty space in which to move quickly. This is the case in deserts and on plains, where there are no trees to slow down the wind's eroding action. Wind is responsible for the planet's great deserts.

# Amazing landscapes

As soon as a new land feature is formed, the different forces that cause erosion begin to transform it. Slowly but steadily, these processes remodel Earth's face in a cycle that may take millions of years. They sculpt an endless variety of new features: rounded mountaintops, natural arches, or breathtaking canyons. Every land feature has its own geological story. In time, erosion completes its work, flattening the once jagged features of the landscape down to sea level.

**The Grand Canyon**

The Grand Canyon is a series of rocky gorges that snake their way more than 280 miles (450 km) through the state of Arizona. The canyon's history goes back to a time when geological events raised the surface of the land more than 4,000 feet (1,200 m). Six million years ago, the Colorado River, which flowed along on the surface of this plateau, slowly began to eat into the riverbed as it flowed to the sea. The river gradually carried away the soil as it cut through the layers of rock, sculpting a magnificent gorge that is approximately .9 mile (1.5 km) high, and about .9 to 18 miles (1.5 to 29 km) wide.

## DISAPPEARING MOUNTAINS

The oldest mountains in the world appeared more than 1 billion years ago. At the time they were formed, they were probably as tall as the highest mountain ranges in the world today. Since then, however, these towering mountains have completely disappeared! Wind, rain, and freezing temperatures progressively ate away fragments of rock, gradually wearing down the mountains until they were completely level. This is the fate that awaits every mountain on the planet.

## Speed of erosion

There are many factors that influence the speed at which a rock changes. Landscapes erode more quickly if they contain rock, such as limestone, that is easily dissolved by rainwater. Erosion caused by running water will be rapid if the rock has cracks or small holes in it. Rocks that allow water to penetrate are very vulnerable to erosive action. The speed at which rock breaks down also depends a great deal on the climate. A warm, damp environment is favorable to chemical erosion because the chemical reactions that can transform rock occur in the presence of water. Alternating periods of freezing and thawing in a cold, damp climate also speed up erosion.

## The evolution of a landscape

The different stages of evolution that a land feature goes through may span millions of years. This is the case for fluvial landscapes, or landscapes that have been transformed by the erosion of streams or rivers.

1. When a landscape is extremely uneven and has steep mountain peaks, erosion takes place very quickly. Streams and rivers dig deep V-shaped valleys into the soil and carry the rocky rubble to the sea.

2. Over time, the landscape flattens out: Mountain peaks become rounder and their craggy slopes become gentler. After several million years of erosion, the landscape is completely flat.

3. A number of different phenomena may occur beneath Earth's crust, causing a sudden rise in the terrain. When this happens, the land feature becomes uneven once again.

4. The process of erosion may start all over again, as rivers dig new valleys into the terrain. In geological terms, it is said that the landscape has been rejuvenated.

# Water's journey

Planet Earth might just as easily be called "Planet Water," because three-quarters of its surface is covered in it. Most of the water is in the oceans, but a smaller portion lies in lakes, rivers, glaciers, and beneath the planet's surface. Some water is suspended in the air in the form of clouds and invisible vapor. Water is always in motion. Heated by the Sun, water evaporates on the ocean's surface and on the continents and is transformed into vapor. The vapor rises into the air, cools down, and changes into the water droplets or ice crystals that make up clouds. The water then falls back to Earth in the form of rain or snow. It either lands directly in watercourses, such as streams and rivers, or penetrates the ground, where it runs until it eventually reaches the ocean. Once again the water from the ocean's surface is transformed into vapor, then clouds, then rain or snow, continuing the cycle.

## BREATHTAKING FALLS

The path of a river is sometimes abruptly interrupted. A spectacular waterfall may form where a river encounters a cliff or steep hillside. The waterfalls of Salto Ángel (Angel Falls) on the Churún River in Venezuela are the highest in the world. They measure 3,209 ft (978 m), two and a half times the height of New York City's Empire State Building!

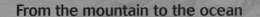

## From the mountain to the ocean

Watercourses begin as mountain springs. Small streams come together and form rivers that grow larger as they flow downhill. Digging into soil and rock, rivers create paths for themselves that lead to the ocean.

**1.** When rain falls on land, some of it seeps into cracks in the ground or into small spaces between rocks. The water trickles downward until it encounters rock it cannot penetrate. It then collects to form a pocket called an aquifer, or groundwater.

**2.** An underground stream may surface along a mountain slope or flow out of a crack in the ground as a spring. In mountainous terrain, the spring rapidly becomes a powerful torrent as it runs downhill.

**3.** At the bases of mountains, streams and torrents come together to form rivers.

**4.** Smaller rivers flow into larger ones, which in turn join even larger rivers.

**5.** The closer a watercourse gets to the ocean, the flatter the landscape and the slower the river becomes. It sometimes begins to wind through the landscape in broad, looping curves called meanders.

**6.** Reaching the mouth of the river, the water deposits its sediment, or remains of organisms and fine particles of rock and dirt that the river has torn away from its banks. This sediment sometimes builds up, forming arms of land that divide the river into many branches before it empties into the ocean. This fan-shaped mouth is called a delta.

**7.** The water finally flows into the ocean.

**8.** The water that evaporates on the ocean's surface forms new clouds, and the cycle begins once again.

# Lake landscapes

The water flowing on Earth's surface usually moves toward the sea. If an obstacle or hollow prevents the water from following its course, it may form a basin. As the water continues to collect, a lake is created. Most lakes are freshwater and contain only small amounts of mineral salts. There are, however, some saltwater lakes. Some contain large amounts of salt because nearby ocean water has managed to seep into them. Other lakes, such as those found in the middle of deserts, are extremely salty. This is because their waters are constantly evaporating under the Sun, leaving behind a high concentration of minerals in the remaining water. A lake may get its water from one or more rivers, which are called tributaries. Without tributaries, a lake may dry up quickly. The water in a lake may run out into one or more streams, called outlets, which follow a course toward the sea.

## LAKE BAIKAL

Russia's Lake Baikal is the oldest and deepest lake in the world. In some places it measures over 5,300 ft (1,615 m) in depth. Fed by more than 330 streams and rivers, this tectonic lake is also one of the largest. Baikal was formed about 25 million years ago and is home to almost 1,300 different species of animals. Many of them, such as the Siberian seal, are not found anywhere else in the world. On its own, Lake Baikal contains 20% of the fresh water found in the planet's lakes and rivers!

# The origin of lakes

Lakes can be classified according to the way they were formed. The origin of a lake is often linked to that of the basin in which its water collects.

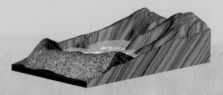

### Glacial lake
A glacial lake forms when rainwater or water from a melting glacier accumulates in a hole dug by the same glacier. Rock fragments carried along by the glacier may form a barrier that prevents the water from escaping.

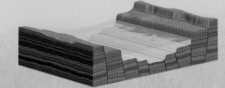

### Tectonic lake
A tectonic lake appears when movements in Earth's crust form folds and faults in the ground, collecting rainwater. These lakes, which are often long and narrow, are also the deepest.

### Volcanic lake
A volcanic lake forms when the crater of a volcano fills with rainwater. This type of lake is easy to recognize because it usually has an almost perfectly rounded shape and steep shores.

### Oxbow lake
A lake may develop from a meander of a stream or river that is no longer being fed by the watercourse. It is called an oxbow lake.

### Oasis
An oasis appears in the desert when the wind moves enough sand away for the water underground to gush out. An oasis may also form when a fault in the desert floor opens up, allowing a stream of water to flow from underground.

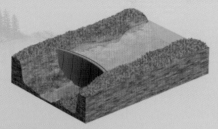

### Reservoir
A reservoir is an artificial lake. Its waters are often held back by a dam built by humans. This type of lake may supply water for drinking, agricultural use, or the production of hydroelectric power.

### From a lake to a marsh
As a lake ages, it slowly fills up with sediment, which is made up of remains of organisms and tiny bits of rock and other particles, carried there by its tributaries. The lake becomes shallower and collects a thick layer of mud at the bottom. The mud, which is rich in nutritive elements, stimulates the growth of aquatic vegetation. Overrun by plants, the lake turns into a marsh or a swamp, before finally disappearing under its vegetation. Although it takes a few thousand years for the ground to become completely solid, the life span of a lake is still considered to be very short on the geological timescale.

# The top of the world

Gently rounded or capped by tall peaks, mountains are the planet's most striking showpieces. They are also Earth's highest land features. Many of these massive, often steep formations are located along the edges of continents. They may form chains, or ranges, that extend for thousands of miles (or kilometers). The principal mountain ranges include the Rocky Mountains and the Andes, which run from North America all the way down through South America, the Atlas Mountains in Africa, the Himalayas in Asia, and the Alps in Europe. The longest mountain range in the world is at the bottom of the ocean! It measures more than 40,000 miles (65,000 km) long and reaches several miles (or kilometers) high. As solid and imposing as these mountains may appear, they are far from being immobile. Throughout their existence, mountains rise, change shape, and wear down.

**Mountains of all ages**
Earth's history is marked by three great periods when mountains were formed. The first occurred more than 400 million years ago. Some mountain ranges in the eastern part of North America are remnants of that period. The second period was around 300 million years ago, when the Appalachian Mountains and some of the massifs of Europe and central Asia were formed. All these mountains are classified as ancient. They are distinguished by their gentle slopes, which have been made round by erosion. The last period occurred barely 50 million years ago, when the Alps and the Himalayas were formed. These young mountains, which are still in the process of being formed, are marked by their irregular, jagged peaks.

Mountain ranges form in a process called orogenesis, where two tectonic plates meet. Tectonic plates are the huge puzzle pieces that form Earth's crust. On continents, there are two main types of mountain ranges. One type is formed where an oceanic plate meets a continental plate. The second is formed by the collision of two continental plates.

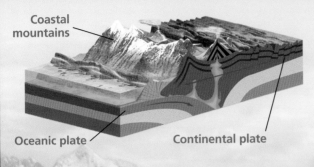

Coastal mountains

Oceanic plate

Continental plate

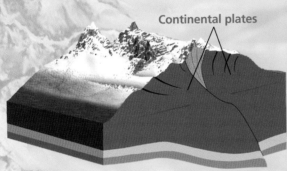

Continental plates

### Between oceanic and continental plates

When an oceanic plate meets a continent, the oceanic plate slides underneath the continent. Rocks and sediment are pushed along and deposited on the edge of the continental plate, creating new land features. As the oceanic plate sinks lower, sediment and rocks build up and may form coastal mountains. A good example of this kind of process, which is called subduction, is the Andes mountain range in South America.

### Between continental plates

Some mountain ranges are created by the collision of two continental plates. The Himalayas, for example, were formed when India and Asia crashed together. The force of the collision folded Earth's crust and pushed it upward, creating a new mountain range.

See activity p. 75

## HIGHER AND HIGHER

The highest mountains in the world, the Himalayas, are still in the process of forming! This range is growing by 4 in. (10 cm) each year. Since the process of erosion is slower than the mountains' growth rate, the Himalayan peaks slowly continue to rise.

# Underground galleries

Caves are underground cavities that have been carved out by natural forces, such as water, rain, or waves. They are found in many different places: in cliffs that jut out into the sea, inside glaciers, and even in the hardened lava that covers the slopes of volcanoes. The largest networks of caves are usually found in limestone formations. These caves often have long horizontal galleries, or passageways, with streams or rivers and deep wells or sinkholes. Caves are not just interesting geological formations. They also provide shelter for many kinds of animals, including bats. Numerous caves have already been discovered, but there are still countless more to be found and explored, much to the delight of speleologists, the experts who study them.

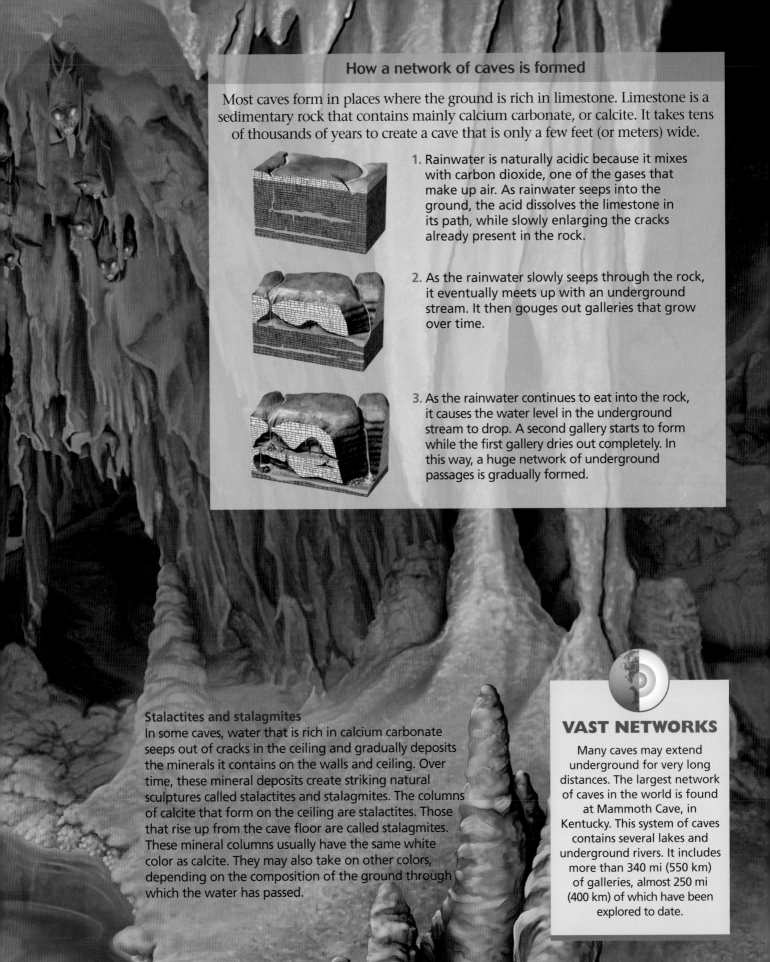

## How a network of caves is formed

Most caves form in places where the ground is rich in limestone. Limestone is a sedimentary rock that contains mainly calcium carbonate, or calcite. It takes tens of thousands of years to create a cave that is only a few feet (or meters) wide.

1. Rainwater is naturally acidic because it mixes with carbon dioxide, one of the gases that make up air. As rainwater seeps into the ground, the acid dissolves the limestone in its path, while slowly enlarging the cracks already present in the rock.

2. As the rainwater slowly seeps through the rock, it eventually meets up with an underground stream. It then gouges out galleries that grow over time.

3. As the rainwater continues to eat into the rock, it causes the water level in the underground stream to drop. A second gallery starts to form while the first gallery dries out completely. In this way, a huge network of underground passages is gradually formed.

### Stalactites and stalagmites

In some caves, water that is rich in calcium carbonate seeps out of cracks in the ceiling and gradually deposits the minerals it contains on the walls and ceiling. Over time, these mineral deposits create striking natural sculptures called stalactites and stalagmites. The columns of calcite that form on the ceiling are stalactites. Those that rise up from the cave floor are called stalagmites. These mineral columns usually have the same white color as calcite. They may also take on other colors, depending on the composition of the ground through which the water has passed.

## VAST NETWORKS

Many caves may extend underground for very long distances. The largest network of caves in the world is found at Mammoth Cave, in Kentucky. This system of caves contains several lakes and underground rivers. It includes more than 340 mi (550 km) of galleries, almost 250 mi (400 km) of which have been explored to date.

# Rivers of ice

In the coldest regions of the planet, the snow never melts. As it collects, snow becomes compacted by its own weight. It turns granular and after several years is transformed into ice. As it slides down a mountainside, this heavy ice becomes an enormous, moving mass called a glacier. Glaciers are found on Earth's highest mountains. Vast continental glaciers, called inland ices, cover most of Greenland and Antarctica. The Greenland inland ice alone covers more than 660,000 square miles (1.7 million sq km). During the last ice age, a period of cold that affected much of our planet, an ice sheet several miles (or kilometers) thick covered almost 30 percent of Earth's land surface. This area included almost half of North America and Europe. With the gradual warming of the planet, most of the ice sheet melted. Today, ice caps and glaciers cover only about 10 percent of the continents.

## RESERVES OF FRESHWATER

Almost 75% of all the freshwater on the planet is trapped in ice caps found at the North and South Poles!

# Glacial erosion

Day after day, the snow that falls on mountain glaciers collects, is compacted, and turns to ice. The weight of the glaciers makes them slide down mountainsides, where they gradually invade valleys and thus transform the landscape.

1. At the beginning, the rocky landscape is dominated by a V-shaped valley with rounded mountaintops. After the snow has accumulated at the top, been compacted, and been transformed into ice, a glacier is born. Pressure from its enormous weight will soon melt the ice at its base and the glacier will start to slide along on a layer of water and slowly descend the mountain slope.

2. As it descends, the glacier invades the valley, tearing up large quantities of rocks and soil that scrape along the valley's sides and base. When the glacier reaches a lower altitude, where the temperature is warmer, the front part of the glacier begins to melt. This frees the collected rocks and soil, which are deposited as moraines. The water at the bottom of the glacier sometimes becomes a lake, with the moraine forming a dam.

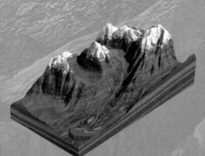

3. After several thousand years, the glacier becomes extremely heavy. It acquires incredible powers of erosion that allow it to carve the landscape. As the glacier retreats, it leaves behind a larger, U-shaped valley with new features like steep, craggy mountaintops and lakes.

## Drifting glaciers

When a glacier reaches the ocean, the power of the waves and the tides breaks it up into fragments. These fragments, called icebergs, begin to drift in the water. Every year, Greenland releases from 10,000 to 50,000 icebergs into the ocean, while the Antarctic releases up to 100,000. Having a surface area between a few square feet (or meters) and several hundred square miles (or kilometers), these huge blocks of ice, mostly hidden underwater, look like giant islands. Winds and ocean currents carry icebergs farther out to sea. Icebergs from the Arctic have been spotted as far south as Bermuda! Constantly battered by waves, sea salt, and the Sun's rays, icebergs eventually melt and disappear.

# Earth's fits of anger

Floating on the planet's surface like rafts on the sea, the gigantic plates that make up Earth's crust collide with one another. As a result of this process, mountains rise up and oceans spread and shrink. The slow and continuous movements of Earth's plates are also at the heart of volcanic eruptions and earthquakes, the most brutal and destructive of the planet's natural phenomena. Added to these are floods and droughts, which bring their own share of devastation.

# The waltz of the continents

Earth's outermost layer is broken into about 13 principal plates, each of them carrying a continent, a part of an ocean, or both. These plates float on the magma in Earth's mantle. This phenomenon is the central idea behind a theory called plate tectonics. According to the theory, several of the features on the planet's surface can be explained by the movement of the plates. For instance, mountain ranges form where two plates collide, and faults form when two plates move apart or slide against each other. Plate tectonics also helps to explain the theory of continental drift, proposed by German scientist Alfred Wegener in 1912. Like many observers before him, Wegener remarked that the continents seemed to fit together like the pieces of a puzzle. From this he figured out that they had started off as a single continent, which broke into pieces and spread apart over time.

## A REPTILE AS PROOF!

The presence of certain rocks or plant and animal fossils on more than one continent proves that continents really drift. This is the case of Mesosaurus, whose fossils were found in both South America and Africa. Because Mesosaurus was a small reptile that lived in fresh water, it would have been impossible for it to cross the Atlantic. The existence of these fossils on two continents now so far apart is evidence that the supercontinent Pangaea once existed.

# A planet in pieces

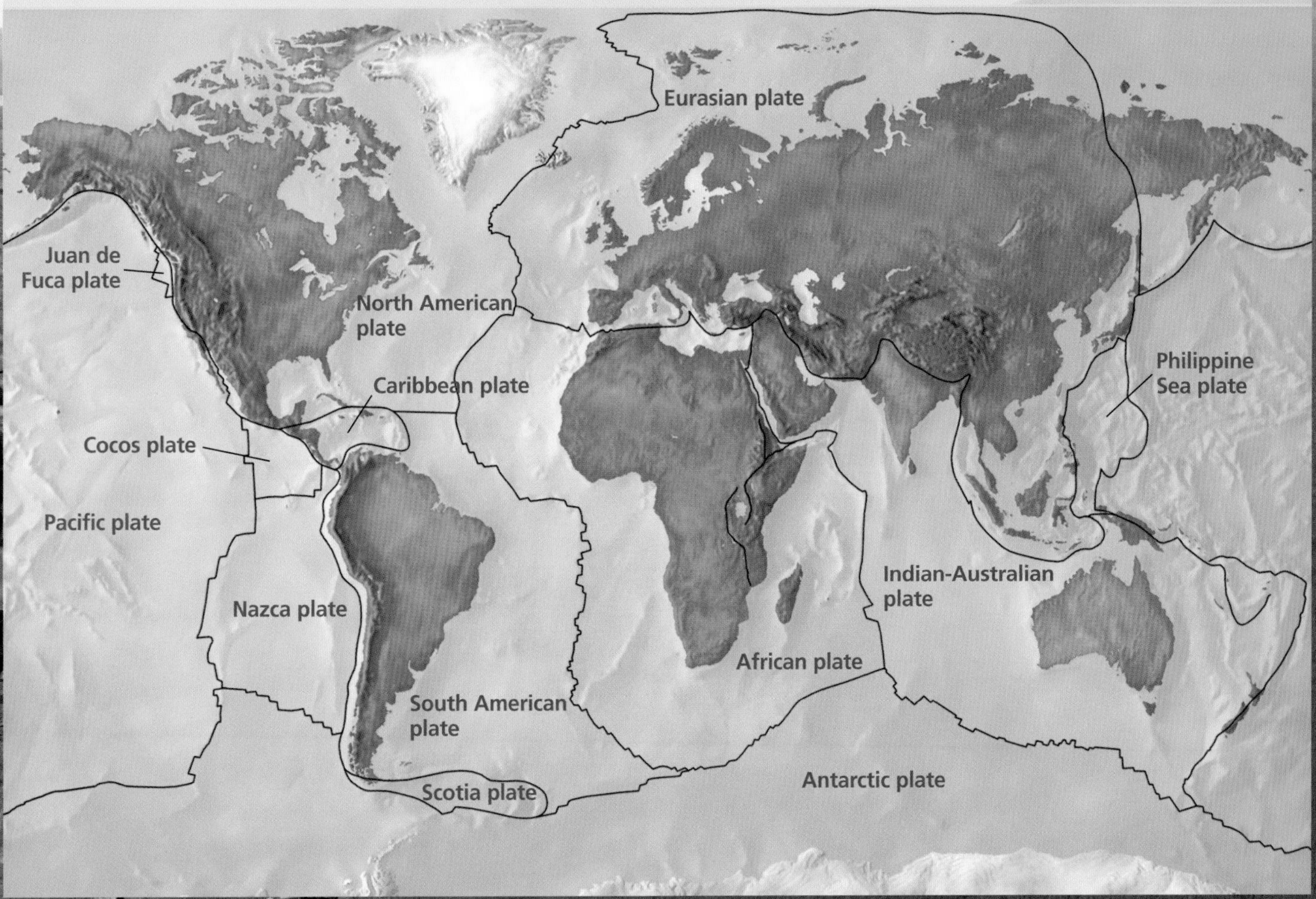

Eurasian plate

Juan de
Fuca plate

North American
plate

Caribbean plate

Cocos plate

Philippine
Sea plate

Pacific plate

Nazca plate

Indian-Australian
plate

African plate

South American
plate

Antarctic plate

Scotia plate

## A supercontinent

About 250 million years ago, all the land on the planet was a single continent, Pangaea, surrounded by the Panthalassa Ocean. Little by little, a new sea, Tethys, separated Pangaea into two continental masses: Laurasia to the north, and Gondwana to the south. Millions of years later, the Atlantic Ocean formed. It divided Gondwana into South America, Africa, and a third mass that included Antarctica, Australia, and India. A little later it divided Laurasia into North America and Eurasia. The continents, as they appear today, then spread apart, except for Australia, which later became detached from Antarctica. The continents continue to shift. As the Atlantic Ocean widens, it is moving Europe and Africa farther away from the American continents by approximately 1 inch (2.5 cm) per year.

# Mountains of fire

There are few things as impressive as the sight of a volcano erupting. Naturally, these mountains of fire are more often associated with destruction and disaster than a spectacular show. Most volcanoes form along cracks in Earth's crust. They are evidence of the intense activity going on deep inside the planet. It is estimated that 1,500 volcanoes have been active on land in the last 10,000 years. Many have not erupted for a long time but could become active again. They are said to be dormant. More than 50 active volcanoes erupt on land each year, shooting out lava, ash, gases, and rocks of all sizes. Volcanic eruptions can wipe out forests, destroy farmland, swallow up cities, and create thousands of victims. An even larger number of volcanoes erupt underwater in the oceans, but these are rarely noticed.

## Two types of eruptions

A volcanic eruption can be compared to opening a bottle of soda that has been shaken. The gases dissolved in the magma are what set everything off. As the magma rises, the gases are released. They push upward, increasing the pressure inside the chimney. Volcanoes erupt in different ways, depending on the thickness of the magma they contain.

**Explosive volcano**
In an explosive volcano, the magma is thick and gluey. It forms a cork that holds the gases inside the volcano's chimney. The trapped gases collect, the pressure increases, and the cork eventually pops, shooting rocks, lava, ash, and gases violently upward. This is the most destructive kind of eruption.

**Effusive volcano**
The liquid magma inside an effusive volcano allows gases to escape easily. The lava flows in a stream down the side of the volcano. It can travel about 60 miles (100 km) at a speed of up to 30 miles per hour (50 km/h) before hardening.

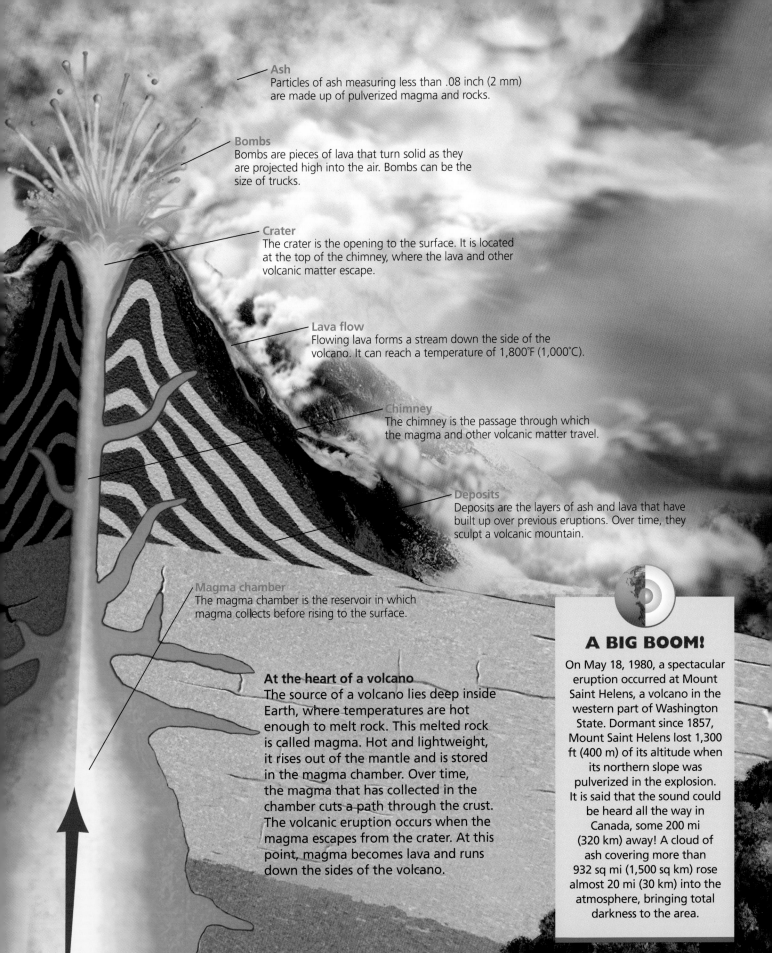

**Ash**
Particles of ash measuring less than .08 inch (2 mm) are made up of pulverized magma and rocks.

**Bombs**
Bombs are pieces of lava that turn solid as they are projected high into the air. Bombs can be the size of trucks.

**Crater**
The crater is the opening to the surface. It is located at the top of the chimney, where the lava and other volcanic matter escape.

**Lava flow**
Flowing lava forms a stream down the side of the volcano. It can reach a temperature of 1,800°F (1,000°C).

**Chimney**
The chimney is the passage through which the magma and other volcanic matter travel.

**Deposits**
Deposits are the layers of ash and lava that have built up over previous eruptions. Over time, they sculpt a volcanic mountain.

**Magma chamber**
The magma chamber is the reservoir in which magma collects before rising to the surface.

**At the heart of a volcano**
The source of a volcano lies deep inside Earth, where temperatures are hot enough to melt rock. This melted rock is called magma. Hot and lightweight, it rises out of the mantle and is stored in the magma chamber. Over time, the magma that has collected in the chamber cuts a path through the crust. The volcanic eruption occurs when the magma escapes from the crater. At this point, magma becomes lava and runs down the sides of the volcano.

## A BIG BOOM!

On May 18, 1980, a spectacular eruption occurred at Mount Saint Helens, a volcano in the western part of Washington State. Dormant since 1857, Mount Saint Helens lost 1,300 ft (400 m) of its altitude when its northern slope was pulverized in the explosion. It is said that the sound could be heard all the way in Canada, some 200 mi (320 km) away! A cloud of ash covering more than 932 sq mi (1,500 sq km) rose almost 20 mi (30 km) into the atmosphere, bringing total darkness to the area.

# Fire from Earth

Volcanoes almost anywhere in the world can awaken and erupt violently, even after being dormant for thousands of years. Although some eruptions are short-lived, others can go on for a long time. Volcanoes are not scattered randomly around the world; they are generally located in areas where Earth's crust is broken or where magma has managed to pierce it. The Ring of Fire, which circles the Pacific Ocean, counts for about 80 percent of the volcanoes in the world. These mountains of fire provide us with the only opportunity to directly study the different materials that make up the interior of our planet. Thanks to continuous observation by the scientists who study them, who are called volcanologists, it is becoming easier to predict eruptions and to evacuate people from a dangerous area before it's too late.

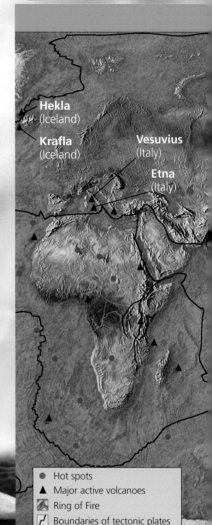

**Hekla** (Iceland)
**Krafla** (Iceland)
**Vesuvius** (Italy)
**Etna** (Italy)

● Hot spots
▲ Major active volcanoes
⬡ Ring of Fire
⤳ Boundaries of tectonic plates

## THE TIP OF THE VOLCANO

The highest volcano on Earth is Mauna Kea on the island of Hawaii. This dormant volcano stands more than 31,196 ft (9,509 m) high. Because its base is located more than 17,400 ft (5,304 m) below the ocean's surface, all that can be seen of this mountain are the 13,796 ft (4,205 m) that rise above the water. If Mauna Kea stood on dry land, it would be 2,168 ft (661 m) taller than Mount Everest!

**Krafla fissure (Iceland)**
The island of Iceland sits in an area where two tectonic plates are spreading apart. It is one of the most volcanically active regions in the world.

**Pinatubo (Philippines)**
The last eruption of Pinatubo completely blew the volcano apart, sending ash and debris flying through the air for thousands of miles (or kilometers).

# The volcano chart

**Mount Saint Helens (United States)**
Mount Saint Helens is an explosive volcano. In 1980, its explosion blew away a part of the mountain.

**Kilauea (United States)**
The Kilauea volcano in Hawaii is located on a hot spot and has been erupting continuously since 1983. It is an example of an effusive volcano.

**Maly Semlyachik (Kamchatka, Russia)**
The violent eruption of Maly Semlyachik caused the summit to collapse, creating a giant crater called a caldera. As it filled up with water, the crater was transformed into a volcanic lake.

Map labels:
Makushin (U.S.A.)
Katmai (U.S.A.)
Mount Saint Helens (U.S.A.)
Maly Semlyachik (Russia)
Fujiyama (Japan)
Pinatubo (Philippines)
Kilauea (U.S.A.)
Mount Pelee (Martinique)
Cotopaxi (Ecuador)
Krakatoa (Indonesia)

## Hot spots
There are particular areas in the world where pockets of magma from Earth's mantle rise very slowly to the surface. These places are called "hot spots." As magma pierces Earth's crust, it collects and gradually begins to form small volcanic mountains in the middle of the tectonic plate. The positions of these volcanoes show the movement of the tectonic plates, which are floating on the mantle. As the plates slide, the rising magma creates a new volcano that slowly burns out. In the ocean, hot spots can be identified by the chains of volcanic islands they usually form. The islands of the Hawaiian Archipelago in the middle of the Pacific Ocean were created in this way.

# When Earth spits water

When rainwater falls to Earth, it seeps into cracks in the rocks and trickles deep underground. In some places, hot magma from Earth's mantle heats the water up to almost 400°F (200°C). The heated rainwater then rises back up to the surface and emerges as vapor or water through hot springs, mud pools, or geysers. Of all these phenomena that occur in volcanic areas, geysers are the most spectacular. The word "geyser" comes from an Icelandic word that means "gushing spray." Geysers can shoot enormous jets of steam and hot water high into the air. Most of these "water volcanoes" are located in areas where magma is close to Earth's surface. Geysers are mainly found in Iceland, New Zealand, and the United States, whose famous Yellowstone National Park is home to more than 10,000 geysers!

**How geysers are formed**

When rainwater seeps into the ground, it may collect in an underground cavity, called a reservoir, located near a pocket of hot magma. The water heats up and gradually turns into steam. As the pressure builds, the steam is forced back up to the surface where it shoots out in powerful jets. The geyser stops spouting when the underground cavity no longer contains enough water or steam. The phenomenon may last anywhere from a few minutes to a few hours. Over time, the reservoir gradually fills with water again and the process is repeated.

## AS REGULAR AS CLOCKWORK

Yellowstone National Park's "Old Faithful" is the most famous geyser in the world. Good weather or bad, Old Faithful can be counted on to shoot up to 10,000 gallons (38,000 l) of water into the air over a four-minute period. It's a performance that has been repeated faithfully, about once an hour, for more than 200 years!

## Volcanic landscapes

Volcanic activity produces a variety of phenomena besides geysers. When underground water and gases are heated by magma, they may shoot up to the surface as mud, water, or smoke, creating some very strange landscapes.

### Mud pots

Gases rise to the surface and form bubbling muddy pools of decomposed volcanic rock particles and water mixed together.

### Hot springs

Water seeping into the ground near a volcanic zone is heated up by the surrounding rock. When the water rises back up to the surface, it is extremely hot. Many hot springs are thought by some people to have healing powers in the treatment of certain illnesses.

### Fumaroles

Fumaroles are vents on the slopes of volcanoes that allow gases to escape. The gases emerge as a column of smoke, as if out of a chimney. The sulfur in the gases makes them smell like rotten eggs.

### Geyser

The jets of steam and water coming out of geysers can reach heights of more than 300 feet (100 m). The tallest geyser active today is located in Yellowstone National Park. Known as "Steamboat," its jets skyrocket more than 410 feet (125 m) into the air.

### Steam

As it is heated, the water slowly turns into steam. The pressure grows, propelling a powerful jet of water and steam toward the surface.

### Reservoir

The water accumulates in underground reservoirs. The trapped water is heated by the hot rock near a pocket of magma.

# When Earth trembles

Earthquakes are produced when Earth's surface is shaken by a release of energy from deep inside the planet. Every minute, there is at least one earthquake going on somewhere in the world. Between 5,000 and 50,000 of them are felt by local populations every year, and many more are recorded by seismologists, the experts who study them. Seismologists use several methods to measure the power of an earthquake. Some take into account the extent of the damage caused, while others, like the famous Richter scale, measure the amount of energy that has been released. Earthquakes in urban areas can be devastating. Since seismologists are not yet able to predict exactly when an earthquake will occur, some cities try to limit damage and prevent accidents by constructing buildings that can withstand vibrations without collapsing.

## A DEVASTATED REGION

The history of China is marked by many devastating earthquakes. The worst of them occurred in the mountainous northwest province of Shanxi on a February night in 1556. Thousands of houses were destroyed and buried under the rubble.

## How earthquakes are produced

Earthquakes are usually produced along the fault lines in Earth's crust where two tectonic plates meet. The underground zone where the earthquake originates is called the hypocenter, or focus.

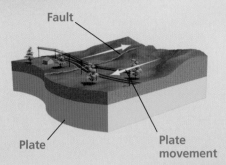

Fault
Plate
Plate movement

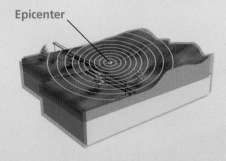

Epicenter

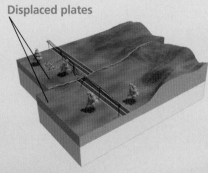

Displaced plates

1. The tectonic plates that make up Earth's crust move from about .5 to 7.5 inches (1 to 19 cm) per year. This movement compresses, pulls, and scrapes the rock along the tectonic plate boundaries, putting enormous pressure on it and building up tension along the plates.

2. When the tension becomes too great, a sudden rupture between the two plates occurs. An enormous amount of energy is violently released, sending a series of tremors through Earth's crust. These tremors, called seismic waves, can set off vibrations from deep in the rock all the way up to the surface. The area lying directly above the zone where the underground rupture occurs is called the epicenter.

3. The earthquake is the most violent and the damage is the greatest around the epicenter. After the earthquake, that region is never the same. The two plates are still side by side but slightly displaced. Bit by bit, the tension begins to build once again.

See activity p. 74

### A wall of destructive water

A tsunami is a series of gigantic waves produced by geological accidents like earthquakes or volcanic eruptions that occur under the ocean. (Tsunamis are sometimes called tidal waves, but they, in fact, have nothing to do with tides.) Tsunami waves can move at speeds of about 370 to 500 miles per hour (600 to 800 km/h). The waves form underwater as a result of the tremors or shocks produced by the earthquake or volcano. The closer the tsunami gets to land, the slower it travels, but the higher the waves become. As the tsunami reaches the coast, it may be a wall of water more than 100 feet (30 m) high—as tall as a 10-story building! This natural phenomenon can be more deadly than the volcanic eruption or earthquake that produced it.

# When the ground gives way

Areas with sloping terrain occasionally see the ground slip away. There are a number of natural causes for this type of movement, which is called a landslide. Among them are major climate changes, which can bring sudden warm spring temperatures or heavy rainfall. Even geological activity deep inside the planet, such as an earthquake or volcanic eruption, can affect the ground above. Landslides can happen as a result of human activity, such as cutting down entire forests on a mountainside or building massive cities on unstable ground. Depending on the steepness of a slope, the nature of the soil, and the cause of the movement, these phenomena may take different forms, from landslips to mudflows, rockslides, or snow avalanches.

### When the ground collapses

During a landslip, a large section of mountainside may slide downward for several miles (or kilometers). These kinds of shifts in the ground often occur after heavy rainfall has hit a mountainous region. The rain seeps into the ground and collects between the particles of soil and the rock, making the ground very slippery and unstable. A section of mud or rock then detaches itself from the mountainside and begins to slide downward, building up to a high speed. These landslides can cause extensive damage. They may block roads, uproot trees, and destroy houses and buildings in the way. A landslide caused by an earthquake is usually the deadliest.

### When the snow tumbles down

An avalanche is a large mass of snow that plunges down a steep mountainside. As the avalanche moves along, it carries with it mud, trees, vegetation, rocks, and more snow, sometimes leaving behind a strip of bare land. Avalanches of wet snow usually happen in the spring, when mild temperatures bring quick melting. The snow that has built up over the winter begins to slide on the thin layer of water lying underneath it, separating from the mountain face. An avalanche can be triggered by vibrations from a passing skier or by a loud noise. As it hurtles down the mountainside, the avalanche is pulled along by its own weight and may reach speeds of more than 210 miles per hour (340 km/h).

## HEROES OF THE SNOW

Avalanches are always a worry in snowy, mountainous regions. Ski stations have teams of people who watch for avalanches and are ready to deal with emergencies. They include ski patrol staff and first aid workers as well as specially trained dogs and their handlers. When it comes to finding a person buried under the snow, dogs are unbeatable, thanks to their exceptional sense of smell and their speed. In two hours, a single dog can comb an area that would take 20 ski patrol members 20 hours!

# Too much or too little rain

Like all living organisms, human beings need water to survive. It is used for washing, drinking, and watering crops, to name just a few things. The amount of water that is available usually depends on the amount of rain and snow that falls. Unfortunately, precipitation is not distributed equally around the world. Some areas barely see rain while others get more than their share. Over time, most people in an area get used to too little or too much. The problems start when dramatic changes occur when they are least expected. Droughts occur when an abnormally long dry period uses up available water resources. Floods happen when watercourses or rain swallow up land that is usually uncovered. These natural disasters are often made worse by human action. Paved roads and cities full of asphalt prevent water from sinking into the ground. As it builds up on the surface, the water ends up causing widespread damage.

**Too much rain**
An overflowing river, long periods of rain, uncontrollable seas, or a break in a dam can all cause flooding. Swelling rivers cause the most floods. Abundant rains and rapidly melting ice may raise water levels in rivers until they overflow their banks. Storms sometimes cause unexpected flooding, along with the extremely heavy rains that accompany cyclones and hurricanes. Besides destroying everything in their path, floods sometimes contaminate underground reserves of drinking water with all kinds of waste. The dirty water becomes more than undrinkable: It also helps spread disease that can infect thousands of people.

**Too little rain**

Many countries that receive very little rain count on small downpours to water their crops. If the absence of rain lasts a few years, it can result in poor harvests and soil that can never recover its nutrients. In regions where the survival of inhabitants depends on agriculture, a lack of rain can be dramatic. If it does not rain at all for a year or more, famine may occur, causing many deaths. In the last 50 years, the longest-lasting droughts and the most frequent famines have been in Africa. The drought that ravaged countries like Chad and Ethiopia from 1968 to 1988 killed thousands of people and forced millions of others to move to more humid regions.

# The environment

All the elements necessary for life, such as water and oxygen, circulate throughout the different areas of the biosphere. The cyclical movement of these precious elements allows matter and energy to be transmitted from one living thing to another, and from one ecosystem to the next. Like all living organisms, human beings are part of the planet's ecosystems. More than other creatures, however, human beings change their surroundings and produce waste that cannot be broken down or recycled by nature.

# The living planet

There are many different and varied environments that support living organisms. These habitats, however, are limited to a thin layer of earth, water, and air, called the biosphere. This layer of life is about 12.5 miles (20 km) deep—from the biosphere's lowest point below the ocean bottom to the highest point in the sky where birds fly. The biosphere is a complex world where plants and animals live in close harmony with their environment, giving and taking energy and matter from one another. This habitable part of Earth is divided into about 10 major natural zones, called biomes. Each biome has its own particular climate and species of plants and animals. The tundra, the boreal forest, the savanna, and the desert are examples of land biomes.

**Ecosystems**
Each land biome groups together several ecosystems. An ecosystem consists of plants, animals, and microscopic organisms that live close together in a particular area. Besides depending on one another, these living organisms are closely tied to their environment. An ecosystem may be as tiny as a piece of rotting wood or as vast as an ocean. Whether they are large or small, ecosystems are not like closed jars. They need to get energy from the Sun and to exchange different substances with their neighboring ecosystems. The delicate balance of an ecosystem may be upset if a single element in it is disturbed. For example, the caterpillars in a forest may disappear if the plants that they feed on are destroyed.

## LOST ENERGY

Each link in the food chain gets only 10% of the energy that was stored by the preceding link. In a food chain in which snakes eat frogs, which in turn eat grasshoppers, 2,200 lbs (1,000 kg) of green plants are needed to produce 220 lbs (100 kg) of grasshoppers. These 220 lbs of insects in turn produce only 22 lbs (10 kg) of frogs, which produce only 2.2 lbs (1 kg) of snakes. In other words, it takes 2,200 lbs (1,000 kg) of green plants to make a snake grow by 2.2 lbs (1 kg)!

## The food chain

All living things need energy to survive and to reproduce. Animals receive their energy from food. Diet varies enormously from one species to the next. Many animals, like deer and hares, for example, are plant eaters, or herbivores. Lions and wolves, on the other hand, are meat eaters, or carnivores. In an ecosystem, all living organisms depend on one another for food. Their relation to one another is like a series of links that together form a chain. In most environments, plants form the first link in the food chain because they are able to manufacture their own food. Most animals are dependent on plants, directly or indirectly. Even carnivorous predators that feed on herbivores depend on plants to fuel their food sources.

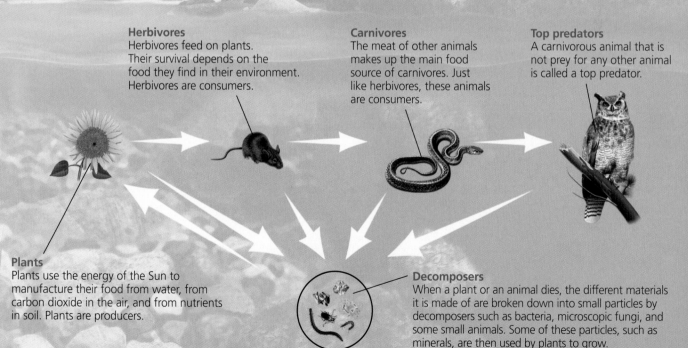

**Herbivores**
Herbivores feed on plants. Their survival depends on the food they find in their environment. Herbivores are consumers.

**Carnivores**
The meat of other animals makes up the main food source of carnivores. Just like herbivores, these animals are consumers.

**Top predators**
A carnivorous animal that is not prey for any other animal is called a top predator.

**Plants**
Plants use the energy of the Sun to manufacture their food from water, from carbon dioxide in the air, and from nutrients in soil. Plants are producers.

**Decomposers**
When a plant or an animal dies, the different materials it is made of are broken down into small particles by decomposers such as bacteria, microscopic fungi, and some small animals. Some of these particles, such as minerals, are then used by plants to grow.

# The planet heats up

The 1990s registered the warmest temperatures on record over the last few hundred years. Studies show that the mercury could rise another 2.5°F to 10.4°F (1.4°C to 5.8°C) over the course of the next 100 years. We know that some gases in the atmosphere, like the carbon dioxide exhaled by all living creatures, can trap the Sun's heat. This natural phenomenon, called the greenhouse effect, helps to maintain temperatures that are favorable to life on Earth. Human activities that involve manufacturing or using motorized vehicles, for example, also produce greenhouse gases. Released into the atmosphere, these ever-increasing amounts of gas add to the natural greenhouse effect, making temperatures rise all over the planet. Even if we do not know the exact consequences of global warming, we know that the climate in many regions will change, affecting the habitats of countless living things, including humans.

**Possible consequences of global warming**
The delicate balance that exists among the different climates on Earth is so fragile that just a small variation in temperature can cause big changes. The melting of the Antarctic and Greenland ice caps would raise the oceans to disastrous levels, putting the coasts of many countries underwater. The melting of the Greenland ice cap would release huge amounts of cold fresh water into the North Atlantic, changing the climate in Europe dramatically. More drought would occur in regions of Africa that are already arid, leading to widespread famine and the migration of entire populations to the already crowded, big cities of the coasts.

## The increase in the greenhouse effect

During the last century and a half, many human activities have contributed to an increase of greenhouse gases in the atmosphere. Intensive agriculture, for example, uses fertilizers that release nitrous oxide into the air. Widespread livestock farming, especially of grazing animals like cattle, produces large quantities of methane gas. Air conditioners and refrigerators use chlorofluorocarbons, or CFCs, which are released into the environment when the appliances break down and are thrown in garbage dumps. Fires and motorized vehicles give off carbon dioxide, as do factories that burn fossil fuels like coal and oil.

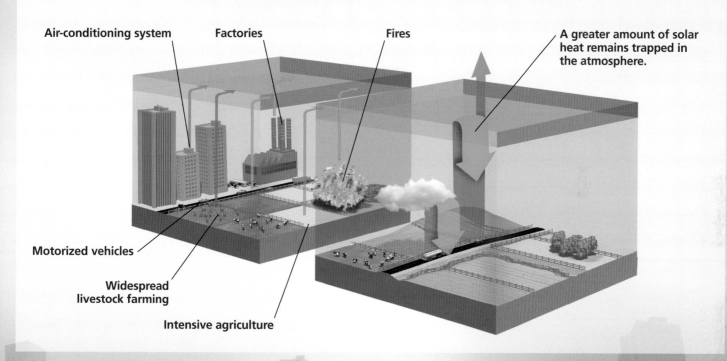

**Air-conditioning system**

**Factories**

**Fires**

**A greater amount of solar heat remains trapped in the atmosphere.**

**Motorized vehicles**

**Widespread livestock farming**

**Intensive agriculture**

### SUBMERGED CITIES

Ocean levels could rise about 3 ft (1 m) between now and the end of the 21st century. Thousands of inhabited islands, particularly in the Caribbean Sea, and the Indian and Pacific Oceans, would find themselves partly submerged. Many coastal areas in Florida, the Netherlands, China, and at the deltas of large rivers would also be threatened by rising ocean levels. Major cities like New York, Bombay, and Amsterdam are expected to be partly submerged by the rising waters.

# Forests in danger

Ever since humans began cultivating land and building towns, forests have been getting smaller. As populations increased, more trees were cut down to make space for cities and for fields to raise crops and animals. Trees also provided wood for fuel, houses, and eventually paper. Even today, trees continue to be cut down, especially in tropical forests. Large forests are needed to maintain the balance of life on Earth. Besides supplying a large part of the breathable oxygen and providing a natural habitat for many plants and animals, forests also protect the soil. When too many trees are cut down, the process of erosion begins, contributing to desertification in some of the planet's dry regions.

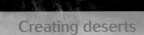

## Creating deserts

Desertification is one of the most serious consequences of deforestation and intensive agriculture. In arid regions where temperatures are high and rain is rare, soil that is deprived of vegetation quickly loses its nutrients. The combination of drought and human activity has transformed some agricultural areas into deserts. The Sahara Desert, which was cultivated 3,000 years ago, is an excellent example.

**1.** In semiarid regions where it rains only once in a while, natural vegetation protects the soil from erosion. The plants also prevent the soil from drying out.

**2.** Agriculture and tree cutting in these natural areas make the soil more fragile and exposed to wind and rain.

**3.** When fields are cultivated intensely, the soil loses its nutrients. The land is then turned over to pasture for animals.

## Protecting the forests

More and more countries have come to understand that it is important to protect their forests. There are many different ways of cutting down trees that can help preserve the natural balance of these habitats. Rather than completely cutting down a forest, forestry companies may harvest only some of the trees and replace them with young plants. The percentage of forests that are managed in this way is unfortunately very low because it is less profitable in the short term. Deforestation continues on a large scale all around the world. An excellent way to contribute to the preservation of these precious habitats is to create forest preserves and to stop wasting natural resources. Managing forests responsibly is also profitable in the long term, because it ensures that there will be a supply of wood in the future.

## ALMOST 47,000 SQUARE MILES A YEAR

Each year almost 47,000 sq mi (120,000 sq km) of tropical forest are cut down. This is equal to an area the size of a football field disappearing every second! Even though these rich forests cover just 6% of Earth's surface, they are thought to contain more than half of all the animal and plant species in the world. Since many new medicines come from tropical plants and since there are many species yet to be discovered, it is vital that these forests be protected.

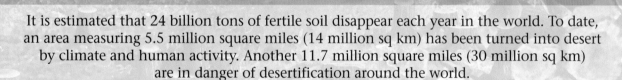

It is estimated that 24 billion tons of fertile soil disappear each year in the world. To date, an area measuring 5.5 million square miles (14 million sq km) has been turned into desert by climate and human activity. Another 11.7 million square miles (30 million sq km) are in danger of desertification around the world.

**4.** Once the soil becomes sterile, which means that nothing can grow, the farmers abandon the fields.

**5.** Grazing on the last remaining bits of plants, the animals finish destroying the soil.

**6.** Completely dried out and without any vegetation, the region reaches the final stage of desertification. The original forest has turned into a desert.

# Out of balance

Of all living things, humans have the most impact on their environment. They change their habitat to suit their needs, more so than most other species. When a growing population finds there are fewer resources than before, it responds by expanding cities and farmland, throwing the natural environment off balance. Many human activities that relate to agriculture, transportation, and industry create different kinds of pollution. Whether they are released into the water, the air, or the ground, pollutants waste no time spreading throughout an ecosystem. The planet's health and future depend on the willingness not just of individuals, but governments around the world, to fight the causes of pollution and to work hand in hand to prevent it.

### Water pollution

The planet's water reserves are constantly polluted by waste from agriculture, industries, and sewers. Since water is always circulating through the environment, it transports the pollutants it contains from one area to the next. A pesticide that is sprayed on a field, for example, seeps into the groundwater, finds its way to a stream, and finally ends up in the ocean. These toxic substances harm aquatic plants and animals, and also infect the food chain, causing certain plant and animal species to become extinct. They can also contaminate humans who eat fish. Even though dumping garbage in the ocean is strictly forbidden, many countries release their untreated sewer waste and dispose of their garbage into the water. In addition to this, more than 6 million tons of oil are accidentally spilled into the ocean every year.

### Air pollution

Many human activities over the last 200 years have been responsible for polluting the air and damaging people's health. Automobile engines and power plants burn combustible fuels like gasoline and coal and allow toxic gases and smoke to escape into the air. Some pollutants help destroy the ozone layer, which is the thin blanket of gases that protects Earth from the Sun's dangerous ultraviolet rays. Other pollutants contribute to global warming by adding to the planet's natural greenhouse effect. Still others help to create acid rain, a phenomenon that has disastrous effects on lake and forest habitats. Air pollution is not limited to industrial areas. Depending on the direction of the wind and its force, air pollutants may even spread to other countries very far from the source of the pollution.

### Ground pollution

Every year, millions of tons of industrial waste, household garbage, fertilizer, and pesticides are dumped into nature. Many of these substances are not biodegradable, which means that microorganisms in the ground cannot break them down. Things like metal cans, glass, and most plastics accumulate in the environment. That is why it is important to recycle and to reuse things instead of throwing them out. Most nonbiodegradable pollutants in the ground come from industries, which emit thousands of different substances. Some of these are highly toxic chemicals that seep into the ground and contaminate watercourses. In spite of efforts to regulate garbage disposal and farming practices, countries around the world are continuing to contaminate more and more of their soil.

## GARBAGE THAT IS NOT GARBAGE

In industrialized countries, the average family produces almost two tons of garbage a year. More than half of that garbage comes from paper packaging, metal, glass, and plastic that can be recycled or reused. Almost a quarter of household garbage is kitchen waste like vegetable peels. This kind of garbage can be turned into compost, a natural fertilizer that can be used to enrich the soil of gardens or cultivated fields.

# FACTS

## Earth in numbers

| | |
|---|---|
| **Maximal diameter** | 7,926 mi (12,755 km) |
| **Circumference** | 24,902 mi (40,075 km) |
| **Volume** | 26.4 x $10^{10}$ mi³ (1.1 x $10^{12}$ km³ ) |
| **Mass** | 13 x $10^{24}$ lb (5.9 x $10^{24}$ kg) |
| **Composition of planet** | Iron (35%), oxygen (30%), silicon (15%), magnesium (13%), nickel (2%), sulfur (2%), other elements (3%) |
| **Length of a day** | 23.95 hours |
| **Length of a year** | 365.25 days |
| **Tilt of axis** | 23.5 degrees |
| **Total area of continents** | 58 million mi² (150 million km²) |
| **Total area of oceans** | 139 million mi² (361 million km²) |
| **Thickness of atmosphere** | Up to 620 mi (1,000 km) (but half of the air molecules are concentrated in the 3 mi [5 km] closest to Earth) |
| **Composition of atmosphere** | Nitrogen (78%), oxygen (21%), other elements (1%) |
| **Highest point** | Mt. Everest, 29,028 ft (8,848 m) |
| **Deepest point** | Mariana Trench, 36,200 ft (11,034 m) |

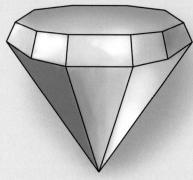

### The largest diamond!

Weighing 1.3 pounds (600 g), the Cullinan diamond is the largest natural diamond in the world. It was discovered in South Africa on January 26, 1905, and was presented to King Edward VII of England. It was cut into nine enormous stones and 96 smaller ones of the highest quality. The largest and most famous of these, Cullinan I, also known as the Star of Africa, was inserted into the king's scepter.

## The Mohs scale

The Mohs scale, which compares the hardness of minerals, is based on a scale of 1 to 10, with 10 being the hardest. Each mineral is classified according to its ability to scratch the other minerals or be scratched by them. Talc, for example, which can be scratched by a fingernail, is rated 1. It is the softest of the minerals. A diamond can be scratched only by another diamond. It is the hardest of the minerals and is therefore rated 10.

|  |  |  |  |  |  |  |  |  |  |
|---|---|---|---|---|---|---|---|---|---|
| Talc | Gypsum | Calcite | Fluorite | Apatite | Feldspar | Quartz | Topaz | Corundum | Diamond |
| 1 | 2 | 3 | 4 | 5 | 6 | 7 | 8 | 9 | 10 |

# The seven continents

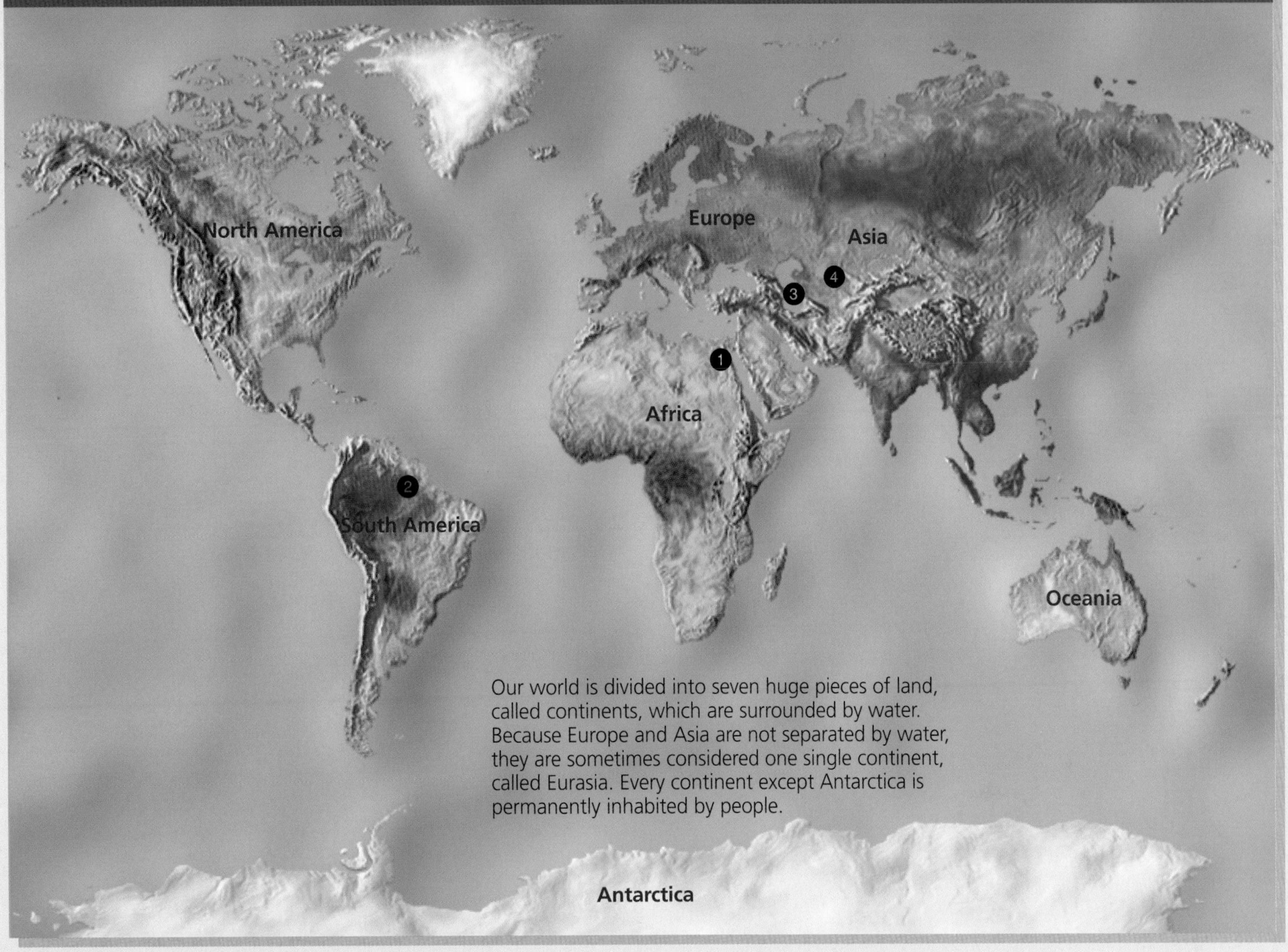

North America

Europe

Asia

④

③

①

Africa

②

South America

Oceania

Our world is divided into seven huge pieces of land, called continents, which are surrounded by water. Because Europe and Asia are not separated by water, they are sometimes considered one single continent, called Eurasia. Every continent except Antarctica is permanently inhabited by people.

Antarctica

## Aquatic landscape records

- The **Nile** ❶ measures 4,140 miles (6,660 km) long. It is the longest river in the world. Its annual floods are an important source of irrigation for the Sudan and Egypt.

- More than 15,000 rivers and streams flow into the **Amazon** ❷, the longest river in South America at 4,080 miles (6,570 km) long.

- Three times the size of New York State, the **Caspian Sea** ❸ is by far the largest lake in the world, with its 149,190 square miles (386,400 sq km). Although this saltwater lake is completely surrounded by land, it is also classified as a sea.

- The **Aral Sea** ❹ is a body of water situated in a desert zone in the heart of Central Asia. It was once the fourth-largest lake in the world. Because farmers are diverting waterways that feed into the lake to irrigate their crops, more than half of the lake has already disappeared. The Aral Sea is now split into two smaller lakes with a total area of less than 13,050 square miles (33,800 sq km).

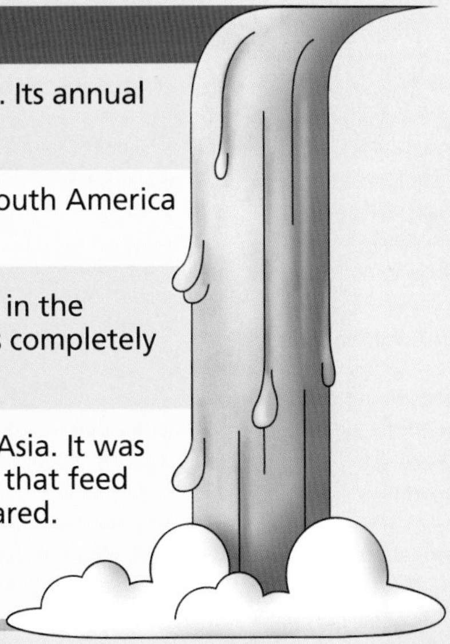

# The tallest peaks in the world by continent

**McKinley, Alaska Range (U.S.A.)**
20,320 ft (6,194 m)

**Elbrus, Caucasus (Russia)**
18,510 ft (5,642 m)

**Puncak Jaya, Maoke Range (Papua-New Guinea)**
16,500 ft (5,029 m)

**Aconcagua, Andes (Argentina)**
22,834 ft (6,960 m)

**Everest, Himalayas (Tibet, Nepal)**
29,035 ft (8,850 m)

**Kilimanjaro (Tanzania)**
19,340 ft (5,895 m)

**Vinson Massif, Sentinel Range**
16,066 ft (4,897 m)

# Richter scale

The Richter scale (invented by American scientist Charles Francis Richter) measures the magnitude of an earthquake—that is, the amount of energy released—with a highly sensitive apparatus. Each whole number in the scale corresponds to 10 times more ground motion than the preceding number. Thus, a magnitude 6 earthquake has 10 times more ground motion than a magnitude 5 earthquake.

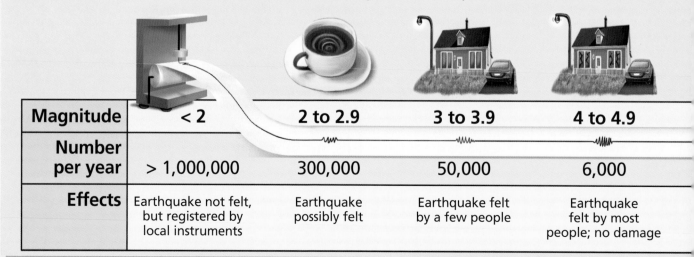

| Magnitude | < 2 | 2 to 2.9 | 3 to 3.9 | 4 to 4.9 |
|---|---|---|---|---|
| Number per year | > 1,000,000 | 300,000 | 50,000 | 6,000 |
| Effects | Earthquake not felt, but registered by local instruments | Earthquake possibly felt | Earthquake felt by a few people | Earthquake felt by most people; no damage |

## The worst natural disasters

- The largest natural avalanches have occurred in the **Himalayas** ❶. Because there are usually no witnesses, no one really knows how big they are.

- The most destructive flood occurred in October 1887 in **China's Huayan Kou region** ❷, when the Huang He (Yellow River) burst its banks.

- The most violent volcanic eruption in human history took place in **Indonesia** ❸ in 1815. The eruption of Tambora was also the deadliest eruption ever.

- The deadliest tsunami in history struck in the **Indian Ocean** ❹ in 2004, when waves of up to 50 ft (15 m) in height (as tall as a five-story building) ravaged the coasts of such countries as Indonesia, Sri Lanka, India, and Thailand.

- The deadliest earthquake of the 20th century occurred in **China's Tangshan region** ❺ on July 28, 1976. Measuring 7.8 on the Richter scale, it caused immeasurable damage.

- The most catastrophic landslide happened in **China's Kansu province** ❻ in 1920. More than 180,000 people lost their lives when many landslides hit the area, following an earthquake.

## Environmental records

- **Mexico City** ❼, in North America, is the most polluted city in the world.

- The **United States** ❽ is the largest producer of carbon dioxide, one of the most abundant greenhouse gases in the world.

- The biggest oil spill in the world was not an accidental one. In 1990 and 1991, Iraq's president Saddam Hussein ordered the army to spill 240 million gallons (908 million l) of petroleum into the **Persian Gulf** ❾ during Iraq's invasion of Kuwait.

- **Brazil** ❿ wins the prize for most widespread deforestation in the world.

- For several years now, **China** ⓫ has been the country to replant the most trees.

- The most acidic rain fell in **Scotland** ⓬ in 1983. It was even more acidic than lemon juice!

- The hottest year on record, since temperatures were first recorded in 1880, was 1998. Another five record temperatures were recorded in the 1990s.

- With an area covering more than 3 million square miles (8 million sq km), the **Sahara** ⓭ is the largest desert in the world.

The World Economic Forum (WEF), an independent international organization, designed an index to measure the environmental performance of 142 countries around the world. The index was based on various criteria like water and air quality, climate change, and land protection. According to the 2002 WEF Report, Finland ⓮ is the most ecological country.

| 5 to 5.9 | 6 to 6.9 | 7 to 7.9 | > 8 |
|---|---|---|---|
|  |  | 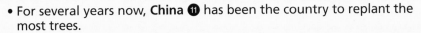  |  |
| 800 | 100 to 300 | 15 to 20 | 1 to 4 |
| Moderate earthquake; some damage caused by shaking | Large earthquake; damage in an inhabited area | Major earthquake; widespread damage in an inhabited area | Very severe earthquake; total destruction in an inhabited area |

## Representing Earth

Since ancient times, humans have been drawing fairly detailed maps of their own little parts of the world. As they perfected their methods, they were able to produce maps that were ever more realistic. Eventually they succeeded in representing the entire globe. There are different kinds of maps, including the topographical map, which shows land features, and the road map, which shows a region's system of roads and highways. Cartography is the group of techniques that are used in making maps. This science has advanced in recent years thanks to the help of artificial satellites. Using photographs taken by satellites, cartographers can draw extremely precise maps of areas that could not be explored on foot or even surveyed by airplane.

### Before there were maps

Before the invention of maps and compasses, voyagers could find their direction on a clear night by observing the positions of the stars. The Pole Star, for example, showed them where north was.

### Earth flattened

A map of the world is a practical way to show the entire globe, but it is not easy to represent three-dimensional reality on a two-dimensional surface: The shape of the continents or the distance between them is always more or less distorted. In order to draw the planet as a flat surface, cartographers use special techniques called projection systems. They obtain an image of the continents as if the image was reflected on an imaginary paper cylinder wrapped around the globe. This technique, called cylindrical projection, always stretches the polar areas. Even if no system is perfect, mapmakers still manage to represent Earth fairly accurately.

### The first maps

The oldest known geographical map is at least 5,000 years old! Fragments of this map, which had been drawn on a clay tablet, were found in Iraq, in the territory that made up ancient Mesopotamia.

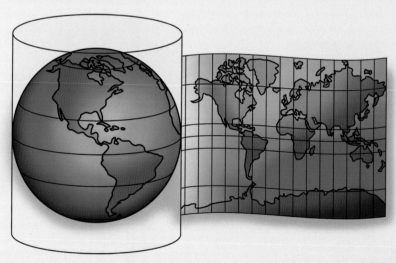

Geographers have created a system of coordinates, or references, for pinpointing any place on Earth, a little like an address. They have imagined a grid of lines running north to south and east to west over the entire planet. The imaginary vertical lines that divide Earth into sections, like the segments of an orange, are called meridians. These represent longitude, which is a place's eastern or western position in relation to the prime meridian line. Parallels are the imaginary horizontal lines that divide Earth into circles that run parallel to the equator. They represent latitude, which is a place's northern or southern position in relation to the equator.

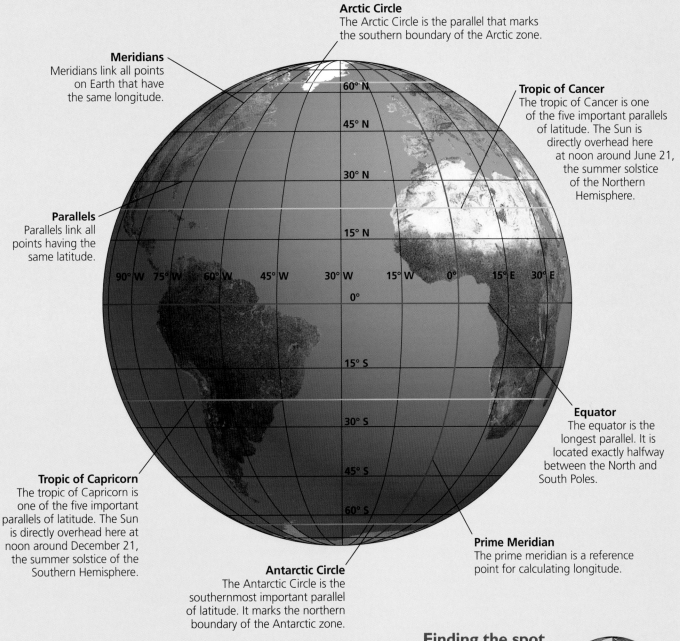

**Arctic Circle**
The Arctic Circle is the parallel that marks the southern boundary of the Arctic zone.

**Meridians**
Meridians link all points on Earth that have the same longitude.

**Tropic of Cancer**
The tropic of Cancer is one of the five important parallels of latitude. The Sun is directly overhead here at noon around June 21, the summer solstice of the Northern Hemisphere.

**Parallels**
Parallels link all points having the same latitude.

**Tropic of Capricorn**
The tropic of Capricorn is one of the five important parallels of latitude. The Sun is directly overhead here at noon around December 21, the summer solstice of the Southern Hemisphere.

**Equator**
The equator is the longest parallel. It is located exactly halfway between the North and South Poles.

**Antarctic Circle**
The Antarctic Circle is the southernmost important parallel of latitude. It marks the northern boundary of the Antarctic zone.

**Prime Meridian**
The prime meridian is a reference point for calculating longitude.

## Finding the spot

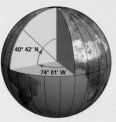

To find the position of a place, one has to determine both the latitude and longitude at which it lies. In the same way that the intersection of two streets provides a reference point in a city, the meeting point of a parallel and a meridian gives the exact position of any place on Earth. These two imaginary lines are expressed as degrees ( ° ). A degree is equivalent to the 360th part of the contour of the globe. Like hours, degrees can be divided into smaller units: minutes ( ' ) and, for even greater precision, seconds ( " ). New York City, for example, is located at 40° 42' N latitude and 74° 01' W longitude.

# ACTIVITIES

## Imitate an earthquake

The extent of the damage caused by an earthquake depends not just on the force of the quake, but also on the type of ground that a house or city sits on. The following experiment will demonstrate why this is so.

### Necessary materials

- A small table
- 2 transparent jars
- Some gravel and some fine sand
- Water
- 2 small toy cars

### Experiment

2. Add gravel to one of the jars until it is half full. Place one of the toy cars on top of the gravel.

1. Place the two jars on the table.

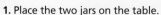

3. Add sand to the other jar until it is half full.

4. Carefully pour a little water into the jar of sand so that the water sinks in slowly between the sand grains. Add water until it is almost at the same level as the sand.

5. Add about .5 in. (1 cm) of dry sand on top of the wet sand in the jar. Then place the other toy car on top of the sand.

6. Let the jars sit for a minute without disturbing them.

7. Shake the table vigorously from side to side to imitate an earthquake.

### Observe carefully

The car in the jar of gravel hardly moves, while the car in the other jar quickly sinks in the sand and water. Rocky soil is much more stable than wet, sandy soil. As a result, earthquakes of equal force can do much more damage to a city built on soft ground than one built on rocky ground.

# Make your own fossil

Fossils are the traces or remains of plants and animals that have been preserved for thousands or even millions of years. The following experiment will show you how to make your very own fossil.

## Necessary materials

- A ball of modeling clay
- A rolling pin
- Petroleum jelly or vegetable oil
- A small object that will be your fossil. A seashell, leaf, twig, or even chicken bone will do the job.

## Experiment

**1.** Use the rolling pin to roll out the ball of modeling clay until it is about 1 in. (2 cm) thick.

**2.** Coat the object with jelly or oil so that it won't stick to the modeling clay.

**3.** Press the object into the modeling clay to make an imprint of it.

**4.** Carefully remove the object and leave the modeling clay to dry and harden.

### Observe carefully
The object has left its imprint in the modeling clay. In nature, an animal or a plant is sometimes buried in sand or silt. After thousands of years, the sand or silt hardens and turns into a rock. By then, the animal or plant has disappeared, but the rock has preserved its imprint, creating a fossil!

# Make your own mountains

Like people, mountains are born and grow up! Try the following experiment and you will understand how mountains are made.

## Necessary materials

- 2 old books (fairly thick)
- 3 balls of modeling clay (in different colors)
- A rolling pin

## Experiment

**1.** Using the rolling pin, roll out a ball of clay into a rectangle about .5 in. (1 cm) thick. Do the same with the other two balls of clay.

**2.** Place the three layers of clay one on top of the other, as if you were making a sandwich.

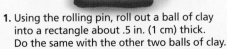

**3.** Stand the books at opposite ends of the clay "sandwich," with their spines touching the clay.

**4.** Slowly push the books toward each other.

### Observe carefully
The modeling clay thickens and folds up as the books are moved toward each other. Earth's surface is made up of gigantic plates that can move in the same way. Imagine that the modeling clay represents a vast flat landscape. As the plates move toward each other, the plain slowly begins to fold up. After millions of years, this movement in the plates causes mountains to grow!

# Glossary

## A

**Abrasive**
Material that wears down, cleans, or polishes other materials by rubbing.

**Altitude**
Height in relation to sea level.

**Archipelago**
A group of islands.

**Arid**
Very dry.

**Atmosphere**
The thin layer of gases surrounding Earth and other celestial bodies.

## B

**Biodegradable**
Can be broken down by microorganisms in the ground or in the water.

## C

**Canyon**
A deep, narrow valley with steep walls usually hollowed out of a limestone plateau.

**Chlorofluorocarbons (or CFCs)**
The gases given off by the fluids in refrigerators, air conditioners, solvents, and aerosol cans, which damage the ozone layer in Earth's atmosphere.

**Climate**
A set of meteorological conditions common to an area of the planet over a long period of time.

**Consumer**
Any animal that feeds on other animals, plants, or microbes (living or dead).

## D

**Decomposer**
Any organism that feeds on vegetable matter and dead animals, helping them to decompose or break down.

**Deforestation**
The action of destroying a forest.

**Desertification**
The transformation of an area into desert through climatic events or human activity.

**Diameter**
The length of a straight line passing through the center of a round object.

**Dike**
A long structure built to hold back the waters of a watercourse.

## E

**Epicenter**
The point on Earth's surface located above the underground source of an earthquake where the shaking is most violent.

**Erosion**
The slow process of wearing down and transforming land features by natural forces, such as water, wind, and ice.

**Eruption**
The ejection of lava, gas, and rock from a volcano.

## F

**Fault**
A crack in Earth's crust resulting in one section of crust moving in relation to the other.

**Fertilizers**
Substances added to soil to make it more productive for the growing of plants.

**Focus (or hypocenter)**
The focus of an earthquake is the zone inside Earth where the first rupture occurs. The energy that is suddenly released by the earthquake originates at this spot.

**Fossil**
The remains or imprint of an animal or plant that lived in prehistoric times and has been preserved in the sedimentary rock in Earth's crust.

**Fossil fuel**
Combustible material, such as oil, coal, or natural gas, formed millions of years ago from the remains of plants and animals buried in rock.

**Freshwater**
Water that contains very few mineral salts.

## G

**Global warming**
The rising of the average temperature on Earth from one year to the next.

**Gorge**
A narrow passage between two mountains.

**Greenhouse effect**
A natural phenomenon necessary to life on Earth. It is caused by gases released into the atmosphere that trap the heat of the Sun.

**Greenhouse gases**
Gases in the atmosphere that trap heat near Earth. Water vapor, carbon dioxide, and methane are greenhouse gases. The release into the atmosphere of large amounts of these gases by human activity leads to an increased greenhouse effect and global warming.

## H

**Horizon (soil)**
A layer of soil characterized by a particular composition and color.

**Humus**
The uppermost layer of soil, made up of substances resulting from the decomposition of animal and vegetable matter.

## I

**Ice age**
A geological time period during which glaciers covered a large part of Earth's landmasses.

**Ice cap**
A dome-shaped mass of ice that permanently covers a large area in polar regions or mountains.

**Inland ice**
An immense ice cap that permanently covers the ground in polar regions.

## L

**Lava**
Magma brought up to Earth's surface. As it cools, the lava solidifies to form volcanic rock.

## M

**Magma**
A thick mixture of melting minerals, more or less liquid, that comes from deep inside Earth.

**Magnetic field**
An area in which a magnetic force exists.

**Meander**
A winding watercourse that runs through slightly sloping terrain.

**Minerals**
Natural, nonliving substances that make up rocks.

## Moraine
Rocks, stones, or other debris carried along and deposited by a glacier.

**Mountain range**
A stretch of mountains linked together and running in the same direction.

## O

**Ore**
A mineral containing a valuable or useful substance, such as metal, for which it is mined.

**Orogenesis**
The process of mountain formation.

**Ozone layer**
The thin layer of gases in Earth's atmosphere that absorb most of the Sun's harmful ultraviolet rays.

## P

**Paleontologist**
A specialist in the study of fossils.

**Plateau**
A relatively flat stretch of land that distinguishes itself from a plain by the deep, narrow valleys that surround it and by its altitude, which is higher than the area surrounding it.

**Primary producers**
Organisms, such as green algae and plants, that produce their own food. Many are food sources for other organisms.

## R

**Riverbed**
A natural depression in the ground, or channel, in which the water of a watercourse flows.

**Rock**
A combination of minerals hardened together.

## S

**Sediments**
Solid materials that have been removed from their original setting through erosion and carried by water, ice, or wind to another location. Remains of living organisms can also form sediments.

**Seismologist**
A specialist in the study of earthquakes.

**Species**
A group of individuals that shares common characteristics and are capable of reproducing themselves, providing offspring that are also able to breed.

**Speleologist**
A specialist in the study of caves and underground rivers.

**Stalactite**
A column of limestone that forms on the ceiling of a cave.

**Stalagmite**
A column of limestone that rises from the floor of a cave.

## T

**Tributary**
A watercourse that flows into a larger body of water.

## V

**Volcanism**
Volcanic activity.

**Volcanologist**
A specialist who studies volcanoes and other volcanic phenomena.

## W

**Watercourse**
Running water that flows in a channel, such as a stream or river.

# Index

**Bold = Main entry**

## A

Acid rain 29, 67
Aconcagua (Mount) 70
Agate 20, 21
Agriculture 64
Air pollution 67
Alaska Range 70
Alloys 23
Alps 36
Aluminum 22, 23
Amazon 69
Andes 36, 37, 70
Angel Falls 32
Antarctica 40, 41, 69
Appalachian Mountains 36
Aquifer 33
Aral Sea 69
Artificial lake 35
Atlas Mountains 36
Atmosphere 7, 9, 16, 26, 62, 63
Avalanches 54, **55**, 71

## B

Basalt 19
Bauxite 23
Biomes 60
Biosphere **60**
Bronze 23

## C

Calcite 20, 21, 29, 39
Calcium carbonate 39
Caldera 49
Cambrian 8
Carbon dioxide 39, 61, 62, 63, 71
Carboniferous 8
Carnivores 61
Cartography **72**
Caspian Sea 69
Caucasus 70
Caves 29, **38, 39**
Chang River 57
Chlorofluorocarbons (CFCs) 63

Clay 20
Climates **26, 27,** 62
Climatic zones 26, 27
Clouds 32, 33
Coal 22
Coelacanth 10
Colorado River 30
Compost 67
Consolidated rock 17
Consumers 61
Continental crust 15
Continental drift 44
Continental plate 37
Continents 14, 36, 37, 44, 45, 69
Coordinates 73
Copper 21, 23
Craters 7, 35, 47
Cretaceous 9
Crust (Earth) 7, 14, 15, 16, 18, 22, 28, 31, 35, 37, 46, 47, 48, 49, 53

## D

Decomposers 61
Deforestation **64, 65,** 71
Delta 33
Desert climate 27
Desertification **64, 65**
Deserts 29, 34, 35, 64, 65
Devonian 8
Diamonds 20, 21, 68
Drought **56, 57,** 62, 64

## E

Earth 6, 7, 14, 15
Earthquakes 15, **52, 53,** 54, 70, 71, 74
Earthworms 16, 17
Ecosystems **60, 61,** 66
Effusive volcano 46, 49
Elbrus (Mount) 70
Emerald 20, 21
Environment 60, 66, 67
Eolian erosion 29
Epicenter 53

Equator 26, 73
Erosion **28, 29, 30, 31,** 36, 41, 64
Everest (Mount) 68, 70
Explosive volcano 46, 49
External core 14, 15

## F

Fault 53
Feldspar 20
Fertilizers 63, 67
Floods **56, 57,** 71
Fluorite 20, 21
Fluvial erosion 28
Focus 53
Food chain **61,** 66
Forests 16, 65
Fossil fuels 22, 63
Fossils **10, 11,** 19, 75
Fresh water 34, 40
Fumaroles 50, 51

## G

Garbage 63, 66, 67
Gems 20
Geysers **50, 51**
Glacial erosion 29, 41
Glacial lakes 35
Glaciers 29, 32, 35, **40, 41**
Global warming **62, 63,** 67
Gold 21, 22, 23
Gorges 30
Graphite 20
Grand Canyon 30
Granite 19, 20, 21
Greenhouse effect 62, 63, 67
Greenhouse gases 62, 63
Greenland 40, 41
Ground pollution 67
Groundwater 33, 66

## H

Hawaiian Archipelago 48, 49
Hematite 21, 23

Himalayas 36, 37, 70
History of life **8, 9,** 10
Horizons 17
Hot spots 48, 49
Hot springs 50, 51
Humus 16, 17
Hypocenter 53

## I

Ice 40, 41
Ice age 40
Icebergs 41
Igneous rocks 18, 19
Industrial wastes 16
Inland ices 40
Inner core 14
Iron 14, 22, 23

## J

Jade 20, 21
Jurassic 9

## K

Kilauea 49
Kilimanjaro (Mount) 70
Kola well 15
Krafla fissure 48

## L

Lake Baikal 34
Lakes 32, **34, 35,** 41
Landscapes 28, 30, 31
Landslides **54, 55,** 71
Latitude 26, 73
Lava 7, 19, 46, 47
Lead 23
Limestone 19, 20, 29, 31, 38, 39
Longitude 73

## M

Magma 18, 20, 44, 46, 47, 48, 49, 50, 51
Magnetic field 14, 15

Magnetosphere 15
Malachite 20, 21
Maly Semlyachik 49
Mammoth Cave 39
Mantle 15, 18, 44, 47, 49, 50
Maps 72
Marble 19
Mariana Trench 68
Marsh 35
Mauna Kea 48
McKinley (Mount) 70
Meanders 33, 35
Mercury 23
Meridians 73
Metals **22, 23**
Metamorphic rocks 18, 19
Meteorites 7
Mica 20, 21
Minerals 16, 17, 19, **20, 21,** 23,
    28, 34, 68
Mohs scale 68
Moraines 41
Mount Saint Helens 47, 49
Mountain climate 27
Mountains 30, 31, **36, 37,** 40,
    55, 57
Mudflows 54
Mud pools 50, 51

**N**

Natural gas 22
Natural habitats 22, 60, 64, 65, 66
Neogene 9
Nickel 14
Nile 69
North Pole 26

**O**

Oasis 35
Ocean floor 14
Oceanic crust 15
Oceanic plate 37
Oceans 7, 9, 32, 33, 44
Oil 22

Old Faithful 50
Opal 20
Ordovician 8
Ore 22, 23
Orogenesis 37
Oxbow lake 35
Oxygen 9, 16, 64
Ozone 9, 67

**P**

Paleogene 9
Pangaea 44, 45
Parallels 73
Pearl 20
Permian 8
Pesticides 16, 66, 67
Pinatubo 48
Planets 6
Plants 16, 61
Plate tectonics 44
Pluvial erosion 29
Polar climate 26
Pollutants 66, **67**
Pollution 66, 67
Precambrian 8
Precious stones **20**
Producers 61
Projection systems 72
Pumice stone 19
Puncak Jaya 70
Pyrite 21

**Q**

Quartz 20, 21

**R**

Rain 29, 32, 33, 56, 57
Rainwater 29, 31, 35, 39, 50
Reservoir (artificial lake) 35
Richter scale 52, 70
Ring of Fire 48, 49
Rivers 28, 31, 32, 33, 34
Rocks 6, 7, 14, 15, 17, **18, 19,** 20,
    21, 22, 28, 29, 31, 37, 39

Rock salt 19
Rockslides 54
Rocky Mountains 36
Ruby 20

**S**

Sahara Desert 64, 71
Salto Ángel 32
Saltwater lakes 34
Sapphire 20
Sedimentary rocks 11, 18, 19, 39
Sediments 11, 22, 28, 33, 35, 37
Seeping water 29
Seismic waves 53
Semiprecious stones 20
Sentinel Range 70
Silica 20
Silurian 8
Silver 23
Slate 19
Snow 32, 40, 41, 54, 55
Soil **16, 17,** 64, 65
Solar system 6
South Pole 26
Springs 33
Stalactites 39
Stalagmites 39
Steamboat (Geyser) 51
Steel 23
Strata 11
Streams 31, 32, 33, 34
Subduction 37
Subpolar climate 27
Subsoil 17
Subtropical climate 27
Sun 6, 61
Swamp 35

**T**

Talc 20, 21, 68
Tectonic lake 34, 35
Tectonic plates 37, **44, 45,** 49, 53
Temperate climate 27
Terrestrial coordinates **72, 73**

Tin 23
Top predators 61
Torrent 33
Tree cutting 64
Trees 16, 64, 65
Triassic 8
Tropical climate 26
Tropical forests 26, 64, 65
Tropics 26
Tsunami 53, 71

**U**

Underground galleries 38, 39

**V**

Valleys 28, 29, 31, 41
Vapor 32, 33
Vegetation 17
Vinson Massif 70
Volcanic eruptions 28, 46, **47,**
    48, 49, 53, 54, 71
Volcanic islands 49
Volcanic lakes 35, 49
Volcanic mountains 47, 49
Volcanism 48
Volcanoes 7, 14, 35, **46, 47, 48,**
    **49,** 51, 53

**W**

Water **32, 33, 34, 35**
Watercourses 28, **32, 33,** 35, 67
Waterfalls 32
Water pollution 66
Waves 28
Weather 26
Wegener, Alfred 44
Wind 29

**Y**

Yangtze 57
Yellowstone National Park 50, 51

## Photo credits

Front cover, children on beach: © IT Stock Free/
PictureQuest; Earth: © Digital Vision/PictureQuest;
mountain: © Bananastock/PictureQuest; erosion:
© Franz Bauer; volcano: © Digital Vision/PictureQuest;
boy on bike: © Photodisc/PictureQuest
Front and back covers, sunset background:
© Digital Vision/PictureQuest
Back cover, desert: © Jacques Bouchard;
marsh: © Corbis/ Magma Photo
Page 16, clear cut: © Alex Mosseler
Page 26, tropical climate: © Caroline Fortin
Page 27, mountain climate: © Corbis/Magma Photo
Page 27, subpolar climate: © Ronald Sladky
Page 27, temperate climate: © Lukasz Gumowski
Page 27, subtropical climate: © Eric Sustad
Page 27, desert climate: © Jacques Bouchard
Page 31, erosion: © Franz Bauer
Page 35, marsh: © Corbis/Magma Photo
Page 36, Appalachian Mountains: © Suzanne Wiliams
Page 41, glacier: © Corel
Page 48, Mount Pinatubo: © Alberto Garcia/Corbis/
Magma Photo
Page 48, Krafla fissure: © Mats Wibe Lund
Page 49, Mount Kilauea: © U.S. Geological Survey
Page 49, Mount Saint Helens: © Glenn T. Space
Page 49, Mount Maly Semlyachik: © Andrei Stepchuk
Page 51, mud pot: © Daniel López Pino
Page 51, hot spring: © John Harbison
Page 51, fumarole: © David Eggleston
Page 53, tsunami: © Pacific Tsunami Museum
Archives/Fumiko Hata Collection
Page 54, landslide: © Neil Moomey
Page 55, avalanche: © Corbis/Magma Photo
Page 57, drought: © S. Colvey/CRDI
Page 62, Venice, Italy: © Michel Bergsma

## Measurements

Most measurements in this book are
written in abbreviated (shortened) form.
Below you will find a key that explains
what these abbreviations mean, as well
as a conversion chart.

| Key to abbreviations | | |
|---|---|---|
| cm | = | centimeter |
| m | = | meter |
| km | = | kilometer |
| km/h | = | kilometers per hour |
| km/s | = | kilometers per second |
| in. | = | inch |
| ft | = | feet |
| mph | = | miles per hour |
| lb | = | pound |
| l | = | liter |

| Conversion chart | |
|---|---|
| **Metric** | **U.S.** |
| 1 cm | 0.4 in. |
| 1 m | 3.28 ft |
| 1 km | 0.62 mile |
| 10 km | 6.21 miles |
| 100 km | 62.14 miles |
| 1 kg | 2.2 lbs |
| 1 l | 0.26 gallon |